Early Childhood Studies

Also available from Bloomsbury:

Early Childhood Studies by Ewan Ingleby

Early Childhood Theories and Contemporary Issues by Mine Conkbayir and Christine Pascal

Maria Montessori by Marion O'Donnell

Language, Culture and Identity in the Early Years by Tözün Issa and Alison Hatt

Respecting Childhood by Tim Loreman

Rethinking Children's Play by Fraser Brown and Michael Patte

Rethinking Children and Families by Nick Frost

Rethinking Children and Research by Mary Kellet

Early Childhood Studies

Enhancing Employability and Professional Practice

Ewan Ingleby, Geraldine Oliver
and Rita Winstone

Bloomsbury Academic
An imprint of Bloomsbury Publishing Plc

B L O O M S B U R Y
LONDON · NEW DELHI · NEW YORK · SYDNEY

Bloomsbury Academic
An imprint of Bloomsbury Publishing Plc

50 Bedford Square	1385 Broadway
London	New York
WC1B 3DP	NY 10018
UK	USA

www.bloomsbury.com

BLOOMSBURY and the Diana logo are trademarks of Bloomsbury Publishing Plc

First published 2015

© Ewan Ingleby, Geraldine Oliver and Rita Winstone, 2015

British Library Cataloguing-in-Publication Data
A catalogue record for this book is available from the British Library.

ISBN: HB: 978-1-4725-0686-3
     PB: 978-1-4725-0682-5
    ePub: 978-1-4725-0633-7
    ePDF: 978-1-4725-1391-5

Library of Congress Cataloging-in-Publication Data
Ingleby, Ewan.
Early childhood studies : enhancing employability and professional practice / Ewan Ingleby, Geraldine Oliver, Rita Winstone.
pages cm
ISBN 978-1-4725-0686-3 (hardback) – ISBN 978-1-4725-0682-5 (paperback) 1. Early childhood teachers–Training of. 2. Early childhood education. I. Oliver, Geraldine. II. Winstone, Rita. III. Title.
LB1732.3.I54 2015
372.21–dc23

                           2014016097

Typeset by Integra Software Services Pvt. Ltd.
Printed and bound in India

Contents

Acknowledgements

Thanks go to colleagues and students at Teesside University and its partner colleges for their contribution to the debates and discussions that have helped to form this book. The book is based on the teaching, learning and research reflections of a number of academic staff who are associated with Teesside University and Early Childhood Studies. Rose Envy, Martin Harmer, Clive Hedges, Sally Neaum, Catherine O'Brien, Donald Simpson, George Stobbart, Jonathan Tummons and Rebecca Walters in particular have all contributed to the discussions and debates that have informed this content.

Rita would like to thank her children, Sarah, Adam and Benjamin, who have supported her throughout and, as always, made the difference. She would also acknowledge her parents, Danny and Mena Trewick, who chose to make her education possible.

As ever, I am particularly grateful for the support of my parents and my wife, Karen, and children, Bernadette, Teresa and Michael. Without them tomorrow would always be a much harder day.

Dr Ewan Ingleby,
31 March 2014

Introduction

This book explores how key concepts within Early Childhood Studies have emerged as essential elements of employability within the children's workforce. Inclusion, enhancing learning, holistic therapies, awareness of the developing child, professionalism and acknowledging the different needs of different children are vital employability themes within today's children's workforce. The book is reflexive in that it explains how and why these key aspects of employability have emerged. Raising awareness of these key employability themes is as important today as it ever has been. Clark and Waller (2007, p.168) draw attention to the 'persistent division' between care and education and the need for strategies to coordinate these services. Doyle (2005, p.13) comments that this can lead to the loss of the centrality of the rights of the child especially when the emphasis is placed upon 'policy and procedure' at the expense of recognizing children's needs.

This is one of the reasons why the book adopts a reflexive approach to understanding where key concepts within the children's workforce have come from. Inclusion, holism, enhancing learning, child development and different childhoods account for many complex aspects of children's behaviour and development. When we are working with children and families, we need to apply key principles of professional practice if we are to endorse best practice and enhance our employability prospects. A major aim of the book is to explain how and why best practice has emerged. This requires a reflexive approach as the central components of professional practice are subsequently deconstructed. This application of reflexivity to professional practice can become a means whereby a balance is offered between what is intrapersonal and particular to individual practitioners alongside what is interpersonal and accepted as being general good practice between practitioners.

Book structure

This book focuses on the emergence of key employability themes within the children's workforce. There are formative activities that attempt to develop cognitive skills so that as well as identifying where aspects of best practice have come from, there is analysis and synthesis of practical and academic content. As well as an academic account of where key concepts of employability have come from, the book's formative activities facilitate a developmental learning process throughout each chapter.

An important theme of the book is the emphasis that is placed on the emergence of best practice within the children's workforce. The book's theoretical concepts are considered to be most useful when they are applied to help understand why best practice has appeared within the children's workforce. This is why all of the chapters in the book contain activities that engage the readers with the content. These activities reveal that best practice and employability have emerged upon reflecting on the best way of working with children and families.

The book's chapters focus upon six main themes. The first chapter explores the importance of realizing that different children experience different experiences of childhood. We do not need to get into a 'time machine' to realize what the experience of childhood must have been like in the United Kingdom centuries ago. Children are experiencing similar challenges in contemporary times in other cultures. This chapter explores the different nature of childhood and its implications for child development. The chapter explores the contribution that ethnography and sociology has made in helping us to realize the differing nature of childhood across cultures. 'Childhood' is a social construction and the differing interpretations given to childhood rest at the centre of these differing experiences.

Chapter 2 explores the implications of the developing child for the children's workforce. A range of theories from psychology and sociology have contributed to our understanding of 'best practice' in helping children to develop. The work of Piaget and Vygotsky draws attention to the ways in which children develop their cognitive skills. The developmental theories of Montessori and Froebel outline how differing approaches to learning and play help with child development. This chapter considers how our understanding of child development has emerged within the children's workforce alongside consideration of how to maximize opportunities for children to develop as effectively as possible.

McGillivray (2007, p.41) acknowledges that the Childcare Act 2006 now legislates for local authorities to work together to meet the needs of children and families. This legislation may be seen as a formal recognition of the importance of working together to meet the needs of children and families social responsibility. Geoff Petty (2009) explains the change in teaching and learning over time as being a change of perception of the teacher from being a 'sage on a stage' to a 'guide on the side'. Petty means that whereas the past emphasis was placed on 'learning through teachers', today's emphasis is placed much more on learning through the facilitation of teachers and teaching assistants. This chapter outlines how and why this change in teaching philosophy has emerged.

Chapter 4 explores how the professionalism of the children's workforce has evolved over time. Key concepts characterizing this shared understanding of professionalism include diversity and meeting individual needs, alongside following ethical procedures such as confidentiality of information. The chapter explores the emergence of a professional children's workforce. The notion of an integrated children's workforce goes back to the Plowden Report of 1967. Today's children's workforce is characterized by professional skills and expertise that have seen education, health and care transform into the concept of 'educare' with a commitment to finding 'joined up solutions' to 'joined up problems'.

Chapter 5 explores how and why inclusive practice has become such a key professional task for the children's workforce. 'Inclusive practice' does not mean 'treating everyone the same'! At the centre of a working definition of inclusive practice is a belief in attempting to meet a range of diverse and at times challenging needs. Societies like the United Kingdom have evolved through reflecting on the nature of social challenges and responding accordingly by providing services for children and families. The 'laissez-faire' notion of leaving individuals to look after themselves has been replaced by a belief in the importance of generating an inclusive society. The chapter outlines key events in the United Kingdom (such as the move away from 'laissez-faire' to state intervention) that have led to the promotion and development of an inclusive society.

The final chapter explores the important concept of the 'multidisciplinary team' within the children's workforce. This multidisciplinary team constitutes the variety of professionals from health, education and care who attempt to meet the physical, intellectual, emotional and social needs of children and families. The chapter explores the merits of the holistic philosophy upon which this approach to working with children and families is based. As opposed to applying therapies to meet the needs of families, the holistic approach combines talents and skills in order to meet needs as fully as possible. The chapter identifies the evolution of this concept within the children's workforce.

All of the chapters within the book are designed to focus upon key areas of professional practice. Handley (2005, p.5) warns against 'seeing children as objects of processes rather than subjects'. The book attempts to provide a comprehensive coverage of key themes impacting on professional practice.

Learning features

The book attempts to stimulate learning through interactive activities within each chapter. As well as these activities there are case-studies and research tasks. The book aims to develop analytical skills through a creative engagement with the content. Alongside the interactive learning activities there are supporting references so that knowledge of key employability themes can be synthesized in relation to these texts.

Professional development and reflective practice

A major aim of the Early Childhood Studies programme at Teesside University is to nurture professionals who are able to reflect on aspects of best practice. This book attempts to facilitate self-analysis in relation to employability and Early Childhood Studies. From this self-reflection there is the possibility of development in relation to meeting the complex needs of children and families.

If this aim is realized it will help to achieve some of the aims of the many Early Childhood Studies degree programmes. The book is based on the teaching, learning and professional development reflections of a number of academic staff who are associated with Teesside University. Teesside University is concerned with 'inspiring success'. This book attempts to contribute to the academic and professional development of those working with children and families. It may be argued that this is one of the finest professional aims one ever could have.

1

Different Childhoods and Best Practice

Learning outcomes

After reading this chapter you should be able to:

- identify how our awareness of different experiences of childhood in different cultures enhances best practice when we are working with children and families;
- analyse the benefits of understanding the different nature of childhood in other cultural contexts when we are working with children and families in our own cultural context;
- critically appraise the contribution made by having a raised awareness of how the experience of childhood differs according to time and space.

Introduction

This chapter considers the experience of different childhoods in different cultural backgrounds. As mentioned in the book's introduction, we do not need to get into a 'time machine' to realize what the experience of childhood must have been like in the United Kingdom centuries ago! The chapter considers how differing experiences of childhood affect child development. The content explores the contribution that sociology and ethnography make in helping us to realize the differing nature of childhood across cultures. Once practitioners become aware of the different experiences of childhood across time and space, they are more able to meet the physical, intellectual, emotional and social needs of children and families. This awareness in turn enhances best practice and employability. The chapter examines the influence of the family on childhood. The central theme is that 'different cultures' (or 'social environments') produce different experiences of childhood. The chapter begins by exploring the sociological concepts of 'structure' and 'agency'. These two concepts examine the extent to which either 'individuals' or 'social structures' determine our understanding of the social world. The content then examines how different cultures influence the family. There is not only one 'universal family type'. As well as the 'nuclear family' of parents and children living together, there are 'extended families' characterized by relatives, parents and children living together. The chapter also explores the impact of history on family types in the United Kingdom. The 'nuclear family' has not always been in existence in this country. It is a family type that has evolved over time. The main theme of the chapter is that differing cultural characteristics make the experience of childhood 'different'. The impact of 'modern' UK culture on the family is just as significant as past cultural understandings of family types. It can be argued that a raised awareness of how culture influences children and families enhances our ability to work according to 'best practice'. This is quite simply because we are able to realize that 'the way things are' does not always have to be 'the way things are'.

Structure and agency

The two terms 'structure' and 'agency' are sociological terms. They explore the extent to which 'individuals' or 'social structures' influence the social world. Structure and agency are also associated with two sociological theories called 'functionalism' and 'interactionism'. In the following table, there is a summary of these two sociological perspectives with a brief description of their key features.

Table 1.1 Two sociological theories

Theory	Key features
Functionalism	Social behaviour is produced by 'societies'. Societies are regarded as being more important than individuals. This sociological theory is often associated with the French sociologist Emile Durkheim and the American sociologist Talcott Parsons.
Interactionism	Social behaviour is produced by inventive and creative individuals. The actions of these individuals are considered to be more important than 'society'. This perspective has been popularized by Max Weber.

These two theories are particularly important because of the influence they have had in (Table 1.1) shaping a key academic debate within sociology. Marshall (1994) argues that the ideas within the perspectives have been informed by the philosophy of Plato, Kant and Heidegger. Durkheim's theory that 'society' is 'greater' than the individual links to the philosophy of Plato. Plato is associated with the concept of the existence of an intelligence that is above and beyond the individuals within society (Audi, 1995, p.618). The opposing idea (that individuals are consciously creative and that they shape the social world) links to the philosophy of Kant (Marshall, 1994, p.265). It is also central to Husserl's interpretative philosophy that is in turn associated with Heidegger's focus on the importance of individual experiences (Marshall, 1994, p.213). This suggests that the concepts of structure and agency can be traced back to these philosophers. There follows a summary of each of the above perspectives in order to develop the definitions within the previous table. Each of the key perspectives is defined, key figures influencing the perspective are identified and central terms within each perspective are explained.

Functionalism

Functionalist sociologists including Emile Durkheim and Talcott Parsons regard society (or societies) as being of more importance than individuals. The theory gets its name from asking about how social institutions such as 'the family' and 'the political system' make society function. The perspective begins from the assumption that every society has a number of basic needs if it is to survive. An example of such a 'need' is the importance of social order. Functionalists consider that social order is not possible unless there are shared norms and values. These shared norms and values can only become widely accepted through socializing individuals. Functionalist sociologists are interested in identifying the ways that order is established and subsequently structured within society. Durkheim is a key functionalist thinker. His work is personified in the sociology of crime and punishment in classic social science texts such as The Division of Labour (1984/1893), Two Laws of Penal Evolution (1899–1900) and Moral Education (2002). The primary focus for Durkheim is not so much the individual but more the whole social body in order to 'maintain inviolate the cohesion of society by sustaining the common conscience in all its rigour' (1984/1893, p.63).

This way of visualizing society results in functionalists becoming interested in the social components that combine to give a society its definition. The components of society (its social institutions such as the family, the health system, the education system and the political and religious institutions) become critically important in establishing social order.

Functionalists are also interested in conflict and social disorder. The forces that are contrary to the established order are understood as being a part of many social systems. Functionalists are interested in the ways in which the social system deals with negative social factors to the extent that they become a manageable part of the social world. The presence of social disorder raises a criticism of functionalism. Taylor et al. (2004, p.15) criticize the perspective for *presenting a deterministic picture of social behaviour*. This is due to the functionalist focus on social systems forming individuals. The reason why this functionalist approach is open to criticism rests in the social disorder that many individuals can experience. If the social system is so omnipotent in the way that authors such as Orwell (1949) have popularized, there could never be the conscious rejection of so many social values that have been highlighted by the United Kingdom media in 2014. This suggests that if one focuses on the importance of the social system to the detriment of acknowledging the importance of creative individuals making choices, one is excluding a massively significant part of social interaction.

Case study

The Tapadar family live in a slum area of Dhaka in Bangladesh. The family include Ayisha, who is a single mother with three children (Fozia (eight), Ehlmad (seven) and Nuruzzaman (four)). Although Fozia and Nuruzzaman are able to help and support their mother, Ehlmad has been involved in a number of episodes of 'challenging behaviour' in the community. She appears to be very different to Fozia and Nuruzzaman. Ehlmad claims to 'hear voices in her head'. This can make her become violent towards others. Ayisha explains the difference between Ehlmad and the other children by reasoning that 'the beauty of children is that they're all different'.

Reflective Activity 1.1

How does the case study contradict the functionalist emphasis on 'structure'?

Feedback

We have said that functionalists are interested in looking at how social groups influence individuals. This sociological theory emphasizes the importance of the 'big picture' as opposed to looking at how individuals create and generate social meaning. The Tapadar family do appear to have been influenced by social factors. It could be argued that the challenging behaviour of Ehlmad is a product of the negative social environment that is being experienced by the family. They live in a slum area of Dhaka. The problem with this argument is that the same social factors appear to have influenced Fozia and Nuruzzaman in a very different way. These two children appear to offer no problems to their mother or the wider community. This appears to indicate that individuals are not entirely a product of social forces. It suggests that the individual characteristics of each person may be a product of forces that are unrelated to wider social environment.

Interactionism

Interactionists such as Max Weber focus on how individuals interact with each other. Weberian theory may be considered as being an appealing lens through which to view early years. The notion of *verstehen* with its implication that the individual should be the primary unit of sociological analysis appears to link to much of the learner-centred pedagogy that currently is associated with early years.

Whitehead (2010, p.6) argues that Weber's concept of *verstehen* can be combined with his analysis of bureaucracy to give a powerful insight into the mechanics of UK social policies. Weber (1968) explains that the word bureaucracy is of eighteenth-century origin and means 'rule by officials within organizations'. The argument is advanced that bureaucracy is the most efficient form of organization that is exemplified by precision, continuity, discipline, strictness and reliability. Weber considered bureaucracy to be an inevitable process in the eighteenth-century Enlightenment world. Allbrow (1970, p.47) notes that one of Weber's concerns was that bureaucracy would become so large that it 'controlled the policy and action of the organization it was supposed to serve'. Weber (1968) outlines an ideal type of bureaucracy that can be summarized as having a specialized division of labour where different individuals become responsible for specialized tasks in pursuit of organizational goals. Weber developed the view that a major feature of modern capitalist societies is the trend towards rationalization. This conveys an emphasis on what Whitehead (2010, p.6) refers to as 'planned, technical, calculable and efficient processes' that are devoid of emotion.

In some respects we can argue that interactionism is the opposite of functionalism. Taylor et al. (2004, p.17) propose that within interactionism an emphasis is placed on negotiating meanings. Individual human encounters are not considered to be 'fixed'. They are regarded as being dependent on the negotiation of those individuals involved in the encounter. Whereas functionalists such as Durkheim emphasize the importance of the social system, interactionists are concerned with the negotiated meanings that develop during the process of interaction. These encounters are visualised as being creative as individual human actors interpret the social system in an inventive way.

Interactionism is allied to 'Symbolic Interactionism'. This sociological perspective emphasizes the importance of how people use symbols within interaction. Speech is regarded as being a particularly important symbolic way of guiding, interpreting and making sense of interaction. Taylor et al. (2004, p.17) are critical of this sociological perspective because of the focus on 'small-scale interaction'. Wider social trends are not necessarily taken into consideration. It can also mean that interactionist studies become impressionistic and localized so that they are open to the accusation that they are unable to obtain global findings.

Reflective Activity 1.2

Think about your own personal development. To what extent do you think that your personality has been formed by the social system? To what extent do you think that your personality is a product of negotiated meanings with other social actors?

Feedback

A way of resolving this 'either/or' dilemma is to think of your personality as having been influenced by a combination factors. In other words, the person is a product of both the wider social system and negotiated meanings with other social actors.

If we adopt this view, neither one perspective nor the other is regarded as providing the complete answer to the question of how our personality is formed. Both of the perspectives are correct to draw attention to the variables influencing personal development. Their effectiveness is heightened if they are used in tandem to account for individual development.

Applying the structure/agency debate to early years

The two sociological perspectives that have been introduced within this chapter can be applied to early years in order to improve our awareness of best practice when we are working with children and families. They offer a number of insights into society and provide us with an opportunity to see how professional practice can be informed by social theory. This raised awareness of the importance of social factors can provide us with an opportunity to base our professional practice on the holistic approaches outlined in Chapter 6. This next section of the chapter considers how these sociological ideas raise our awareness of different childhoods in different cultures.

Functionalism and early years

In the previous section of the chapter we defined functionalism as being a sociological perspective that is concerned with how social systems maintain the consensus. This macro approach focuses on the bigger social picture by drawing attention to the impact of wider society on children and families. The emphasis is placed on how children and families are affected by social structures such as the education system, the health system and the political system. In the United Kingdom there was relatively little statutory support offered to children and families prior to 1946. This pivotal date is the time when the welfare state became such an important part of UK social policy. William Beveridge's notion of a welfare state looking after the needs of children and families from birth until death became a dominant idea within UK society from 1946 onwards. The welfare state led to the introduction of the NHS, social security and social services. There was a formal recognition that the wider social system has a massive impact upon the lives of children and families.

It is important for early years practitioners to acknowledge that the social system has a massive impact on the life chances of children and families. It can be argued that the relatively affluent life style enjoyed by many UK people today is a product of the welfare state. It is important for early years practitioners to become as fully aware as possible of the state services that are available to help children and families. As opposed to accepting that responsibility rests with individuals to be 'self-reliant', it is important to acknowledge that life chances are heavily influenced by the type of society that has been created. This argument is justified by considering the many problems that are experienced by children and families living in countries that do not have a welfare state. If the social system is underdeveloped so that individual families become accountable for their life chances there are fewer opportunities for those children and families who are unable to look after their own interests.

Early years practitioners need to be aware of the importance of having robust social agencies that are able to plan for and coordinate effective health care and education. This does not mean that it is necessary for early years practitioners to become political activists! It is more of a need to learn the lessons of history. The welfare state has improved the life chances of many children and families so it is important to acknowledge the importance of wider social structures being able to help those who cannot help themselves.

The following case study example outlines the ways in which the functionalist awareness of the social system can be applied to early years.

Case study

The Kaur family arrived in the United Kingdom after spending a number of years living in Delhi. Mr and Mrs Kaur have three children aged seven, five and three. The family have become used to being reliant on each other because of the difficulties with the infrastructure in Delhi. They used to live in a poor district of the city. There were no shops in this area, no running water and no school for the children until last year. A Roman Catholic missionary organization established a school for the children and the benefits of a basic education persuaded the Kaurs to move to the United Kingdom. The family are now able to enjoy a much more robust infrastructure. There is an established health care and education system in the United Kingdom alongside the presence of employment opportunities. The Kaur family has started to attend mass at a local Catholic Church and their children already receive a number of social and educational benefits from being part of this religious community. Each Sunday there is a 'children's liturgy' and the children get to use pens, paper, books and musical instruments. One of the parishioners is a foreman in a local factory and he immediately alerted Mr Kaur to the possibility of 'casual labour'. The Kaurs think that their life opportunities are dramatically different within a social system that appears to offer so many opportunities.

Reflective Activity 1.3

How can functionalism be applied to this case study?

Feedback

In the case study about the Tapadar family, we said that functionalists are not able to explain every aspect of child development because there are 'non-social' factors that also influence children. The above case study does, however, reveal the potential importance that a child's social environment can have on its individual development. When a social system has a poorly developed infrastructure, this is likely to have profound consequences for the child's development. Once the Kaur family move to a society with an improved infrastructure, there are more opportunities for the family and these opportunities (both economic and social) help the children's physical, intellectual, emotional and social development.

Interactionism and early years

In contrast to functionalism, the interactionist school of thought emphasizes the importance of individuals. There is less focus on macro sociological structures and much more attention paid to the ways in which individuals negotiate meaning during their social encounters. This sociological perspective is important for early years because it reinforces the importance of meeting the individual needs of children. The interactionist approach to sociology would endorse any practice that aims to treat children as individuals, with the potential to grow and develop as long as this opportunity is presented to them. Even the word 'sociology' appears to emphasize the importance of studying groups of individuals as opposed to focusing on the meanings that are negotiated by social actors. To apply an analogy, it is as if the 'individual trees' are being missed because of the focus on the 'wider wood'. It can be argued that effective early years practice cannot be characterized by looking at major social structures because the individual needs of children and families are likely to be missed if this is the prevalent approach to practice. The interactionist approach to sociology begins by asking how individuals interpret the social world and in turn negotiate social meanings. If early years practitioners adopt a similar philosophy, the individual child and their rights is likely to become central to practice. This theme is emphasized in Nigel Parton's (2005) book. It is considered to be vital that children's individual needs are central to practice if quality child care provision is to be given.

If an interactionist approach to early years work is adopted, it is also more likely that the creativity of children will be acknowledged and incorporated into best practice when we are working with children and families. It can be argued that an interactionist perspective may be more aware of the importance of 'free-play' because of the emphasis that is put on each child nurturing their individual creativity. Play techniques that stimulate the child's imagination are also likely to be considered to be important to children's growth and development if one adopts an interactionist perspective. This is due to the emphasis that is placed on meanings being negotiated by creative individuals. Some of the benefits of an interactionist approach to early years practice are outlined in the following case study.

Case study

Alex has recently completed a PGCE and she is in her first teaching post in a primary school. Alex has a child in her reception class who is from Sweden. The child and her parents have experienced a different education system in Sweden. There is an emphasis placed on 'play' with children being encouraged to learn 'at their own pace'. Alex is aware that the emphasis placed on 'literacy' and 'reading' in early years in the United Kingdom may appear to be contradictory to the Swedish emphasis that is placed on children 'learning at their own pace'. Alex has found that she has to adapt her teaching style in order to meet the individual needs of her Swedish pupil (Anna). As part of her MA in Education, Alex attended a module that explored how the education system in Sweden differs from that in the United Kingdom. She found that this was an invaluable part of her study. It has made Alex much more aware of how to become a reflective practitioner who is able to take the learning needs of other children into consideration.

Reflective Activity 1.4

How can interactionism be applied to this case study?

Feedback

We have stressed that interactionists emphasize the importance of individuals and their ability to create and negotiate social meanings. The importance of ensuring that cultural factors are acknowledged within teaching and learning appears to support what interactionism says. As opposed to emphasizing the importance of the 'national curriculum', interactionism places an emphasis on the importance of the individual. In this case study, Anna's cultural background is taken into consideration to ensure that best practice occurs in learning and teaching.

Different cultures and different families

Haralambos and Holborn (1995, p.317) cite George Peter Murdock's (1949) work in addressing the question 'is the family a universal social institution?' Murdock based his research on 250 societies. These families ranged from small 'hunter gatherer bands' to 'large-scale industrial societies', with the overwhelming conclusion being that every human society is characterized by 'the family'. Murdock understands the family to mean 'blood relations living together'. He uses his research to conclude that 'the family' is a 'universal social institution'.

Reflective Activity 1.5

Write out a definition of 'the family'.

Feedback

The saying 'blood is thicker than water' is helpful in understanding why relatives are often regarded as being more important than 'friends'. Being 'related to someone' implies a biological link that can be the basis of a sense of 'obligation'. You might have defined the family as 'individuals related by blood who share a sense of duty towards each other'. Haralambos and Holborn (1995, p.317) cite Murdock's (1949) definition of the family as a 'social group characterized by common residence, economic cooperation and reproduction' as a workable definition of 'the family'.

> Murdock's (1949) work can be used to argue that the family is usually present in human societies. It can also be suggested that the type of family varies according to the social group's cultural characteristics. This variation in family type has interested social scientists for a number of years. The significance for early years is that the type of family appears to have an important influence on the experience of childhood.
>
> Murdock (1949) considers the nuclear family to be especially important in human societies. His research identified that nuclear families were present in each of the 250 societies in his study. It can, however, be argued that despite the importance of the nuclear family, there are examples of other types of societies who have different family arrangements and this has an inevitable influence on the experience of childhood. Becoming aware of these cultural differences is an important aspect of enhancing your best professional practice when you are working with other children and families.

The Nayar experience of childhood

Kathleen Gough's (1959) work on the Nayar of Kerala in southern India reveals that different understandings of the family exist in other cultures. These different understandings can have a profound impact upon childhood experiences. Gough's anthropological account of Nayar society reveals that before puberty, Nayar girls were ritually married to suitable Nayar men. Following this ritual marriage, the 'husband' did not live with his 'wife' and he was under no obligation to have any contact with her whatsoever. The only obligation that the wife had was to attend her husband's funeral and mourn his death.

Upon reaching puberty, a Nayar girl would take a number of visiting men or 'sandbanham' husbands. Nayar men would often be away from their villages as 'professional warriors'. During this time they would visit villages and visit any number of Nayar women who had been ritually married. The 'sandbanham' husband would arrive at the home of one of his wives in the evening, have sexual intercourse with her and leave before breakfast the next day. Gough reports that whereas men could have unlimited numbers of 'sandbanham' wives, women were limited to having no more than twelve visiting husbands.

The Nayar case reported by Kathleen Gough provides a very different experience of family life to most societies. The 'couple' were not in a conventional lifelong union. Moreover, 'sandbanham' husbands had no obligation towards the offspring of their wives. The 'father' of a child was expected to pay a fee of 'cloth and vegetables' to the midwife attending the childbirth, but the 'father' was not necessarily the biological father of the child. When a Nayar woman became pregnant, the only expectation was that 'someone' acknowledged that they were the child's father. The role of a father appears to be more of a social convention of 'acknowledgement' as a child's father had no social or financial obligations.

Gough also reveals that in Nayar society, husbands and wives did not form an economic union. Although husbands might give their wives gifts, there was no expectation for a husband to 'provide for his wife'. Moreover, Gough reports that if a husband did try to 'provide for his wife', this was frowned upon within Nayar society. The economic unit was made up of brothers, sisters, sisters' children and daughters' children. The leader of this social unit was the eldest male.

Nayar society is described as being 'matrilineal' by Haralambos and Holborn (1995, p.318). The family groupings were based on female biological relatives and marriage provided no role in establishing households, socializing children or meeting economic needs. Sexual relations were socially sanctioned between couples who neither lived together nor cooperated together economically. Haralambos and Holborn (1995, p.318) argue that the implications of Gough's work are that either Murdock's definition of the family is too narrow or that the family is not universal.

Reflective Activity 1.6

What do you think the experience of childhood would be like for Nayar children? What do you think are the advantages and disadvantages of this experience of childhood compared to our culture?

Feedback

Nayar children have a very different relationships with their biological fathers compared to many children in our own society. The Nayar are described as being 'a matrilineal society'. Women were formally acknowledged as being of central importance to Nayar society. Nayar children did not have close relationships with their biological fathers in comparison to the expectations of many children in UK society. If you think that children's growth and development is enhanced by a close emotional relationship with a biological father, you could argue that Nayar children experienced a less favourable family environment in comparison to many families living in the United Kingdom. It can also be argued that a close emotional relationship between a biological father and his children can often be an 'ideal' as opposed to a 'reality'. The experiences of many UK children can resemble those that have been so powerfully phrased by DH Lawrence (1956) in novels such as *Sons and Lovers*. Lawrence grew up in a working-class mining community in the midlands of England in the late twentieth century. His recollections of living in a family experiencing domestic violence from the male head of the family might belong to an earlier century, but they are still relevant to what is happening in England in 2014. The harrowing scenes of domestic violence that Lawrence portrays are less likely to appear in Nayar society as their experience of childhood is not shaped by the nuclear family.

The next section of the chapter continues to develop the theme that childhood experiences differ according to family type. As well as 'cultural differences', 'the family' has changed over time. The experiences of childhood are linked to historical perspectives. The implication suggests that different times have been characterized by different types of family. Awareness of the changing nature of the family enhances your opportunity to deliver best practice when you are working with children and families as you are more likely to become sensitive to individual needs.

Different times and different families

As well as differing according to place, the family also differs according to 'time'. In other words, different times in history have been characterized by different forms of family. Haralambos and Holborn (1995, p.334) make this point by arguing that pre-industrial societies can have very different family types compared to industrial societies. These are what are referred to as 'pre-industrial families'.

Pre-industrial families

Anthropologists such as I.M. Lewis (1981) argue that kinship relationships are especially important within the social life of many pre-industrial societies. This is because individual families become part of wider kinship relationships and the childhood experiences of family life can be contrasted with those experiences of children in industrial societies. Kinship groups are often linked by mutual rights and obligations. This sense of obligation is revealed by Haralambos and Holborn (1995, p.335), who cite the reflection of a Pomo Indian of northern California to draw attention to the importance of the family for children in pre-industrial societies. As opposed to relying on 'the state', it is 'the family' who are considered as being 'all important'.

As opposed to experiencing childhood within 'nuclear families', many pre-industrial children live in what Haralambos and Holborn (1995, p.335) refer to as 'classic extended families'. These families are characterized by the 'extended family' being of particular importance. Haralambos and Holborn (1995, p.335) argue that the traditional Irish patriarchal farming family that sees property passing down through male relatives is an example of this form of pre-industrial family. Within this family type, social and economic roles are amalgamated. The typical 'extended family' consists of a male head, his wife and children, his parents, and unmarried brothers and sisters. The family work together as a 'production unit' so that the family can maintain economic sustenance.

Reflective Activity 1.7

What do you think the experience of childhood would be like for children living in pre-industrial families? What do you think would be the advantages and disadvantages of this experience of childhood compared to the experience of childhood today in our culture?

Feedback

You could argue that 'family breakdown' is a characteristic of family life in modern industrial societies. You could also argue that such family breakdown is less likely to be a characteristic of pre-industrial societies because families such as the Irish extended family relied on each other for economic sustenance. The experience of childhood will be very different for children in these families. The choice of 'staying together' or 'separating' is a less likely option in this situation of economic dependence. In pre-industrial societies such as rural Ireland, children may not have had the material benefits that many children in industrial societies enjoy. It can also be argued that such children may not have experienced the 'pain of separation' that many children in industrial societies experience. As with all societies, there will be both positive and negative aspects of 'childhood experience'. It would appear to be the case that it is important to make sure that 'childhood' is not defined as 'absolutely better' or 'absolutely worse' according to time! Awareness of this point is likely to make your working practice with children and families characterized by best practice because you will be able to respond to individual cultural needs.

Was the typical pre-industrial society family 'extended'?

Peter Laslett (1972) has contributed to our understanding of how 'time' influences family type. Laslett, a Cambridge historian, has popularized the nature of family size and composition in pre-industrial England. He discovered that from 1564 to 1821 there were only 10 per cent of households who had kin beyond the nuclear family living with them. This percentage is the same for England in 1966. Laslett also presents data from America to support his argument that pre-industrial societies are not necessarily characterized by 'extended families'. According to Laslett, the idea that a large extended family gave way to a nuclear family following industrialization is a 'myth'. If this is true, it might mean that there are more similarities in children's experiences in pre-industrial times than we might immediately assume. Make sure that you do not assume that the media are right in their portrayal of childhood experiences being so different in pre-industrial times!

Laslett developed his research by investigating pre-industrial family size in other countries. He arrived at the conclusion that the nuclear family was the typical family type in northern France, the Netherlands, Belgium, Scandinavia, parts of Italy and Germany. This family type contrasted with Eastern Europe, Russia and Japan where the extended family was more common. Laslett has used these findings to argue that the presence of the nuclear family was one of the key factors that led to Western Europe becoming the first area of the world to experience an 'industrial revolution'. This finding is supported by Berger (1983), who argues that the nuclear family facilitated 'modernity' because it encouraged patterns of thought that were conducive to industrial development. The argument runs that nuclear families encourage individuals to be self-reliant and independent. These qualities are considered to be essential if 'industrial entrepreneurs' are to flourish.

Haralambos (1996, p.338) argues that Laslett's work is important because it 'exploded the myth' that the extended family was the typical family type for pre-industrial Britain. Haralambos goes on to argue that although Laslett's work does make a contribution to understanding childhood experiences, his conclusions need to be viewed with some caution. Michael Anderson (1980) has identified some contradictory evidence in Laslett's own research. Anderson argues that although the average household size may have been under five people, the majority of the population of pre-industrial Britain (53 per cent) lived in households of six or more people. Anderson also argues that in Sweden, extended families were very common and that family type between social groups in the United Kingdom evidenced considerable variation. As an example of this variation, Anderson discovered that 'gentry' and 'yeoman' farmers tended to have much larger households than the average. This is one of the reasons why Anderson is critical of the idea of the 'Western nuclear family'. He argues that it is more sensible to accept that pre-industrial Europe was characterized by 'family diversity' without any one type of family being predominant. If this is the case, it suggests that childhood experiences in pre-industrial times will vary according to what is accepted as being the 'ideal family type'. This reinforces a theme of this chapter that the diversity of human societies leads to differing and highly interesting interpretations of childhood. Becoming aware of these differences enables us to meet the individual needs of children and families and mirror best professional practice.

Reflective Activity 1.8

Do you think that 'family type' is the most important factor influencing children's experience of childhood?

Feedback

A theme within Chapter 6 of this book is the importance of the environment on child development. You could argue that the 'platform' for child development is 'the family'. Children are usually born into families and these familial experiences become crucial for children's development. 'Family type' or the sort of family environment experienced by the child can become critical to their development. A child's physical, intellectual, emotional and social development is likely to be determined by their familial environment. You might argue that 'genes, chromosomes, and hormones' are also critical factors in a child's development. In other words, the 'biological nature' of a child is also of crucial importance to its development. It can be difficult to identify which of these two factors is the most important for child development. You may choose to argue that 'biology' and 'family type' both have a critical role to play in how the child develops.

UK families: Modern families in a modern culture

Investigating children's experiences of childhood in other cultures and through history reveals the complexity of childhood through time and space. You could also argue that the experience of childhood in the United Kingdom today is also characterized by much diversity. This point is made by Haralambos and Holborn (1995, p.346). There is what Leach (1997) refers to as the 'cereal packet image' of the family. Leach uses this image to describe the 'typical family' being featured in some UK cereal advertisements. The image is of a happily married couple who have two children with the implication being that this type of family is somehow 'ideal'.

The idea that this 'cereal packet image' family is 'real' can be challenged if you consider some of the research that has been completed on the family. Haralambos and Holborn (1995, p.347) make this point when they cite the research completed by Robert and Rhona Rapoport (1978). The findings of their research identified that only 24 per cent of families consisted of married couples, children and one 'breadwinner'. In other words, the United Kingdom has witnessed a decline in the number of households that are constituted of married couples and dependent children. Haralambos and Holborn (1995, p.347) quantify this argument by stating that the percentage of UK households containing married couples and dependent children declined from 38 per cent in 1961 to 24 per cent in 1992. This point is supported by the increase of single person households. Haralambos and Holborn (1995, p.347) record that the figure changed from 2.5 per cent in 1961 to 10.1 per cent in 1992. The Rapoports (1978) consider this trend to be similar in many other European countries. It is also a trend that has continued through to 2013. Social Trends (2010) reveals that the proportion of children living in families with two married parents fell from 72 per cent in 1997 to 63 per cent in 2009.

The Social Trends (2010) findings reveal other key statistics about the nature of family life. From 2004 to 2007, the number of marriages fell for the third consecutive year. The statistics also show that the number of people living in a typical household fell from an average of 3.1 in 1961 to 2.4 people in 2009. This suggests that children's experience of childhood will be very different in general compared with the pre-industrial families that were exemplified in the previous sections of the chapter.

Reflective Activity 1.9

The Social Trends statistics reveal that marriage is becoming less popular and that increasing numbers of children are living in single-parent families. What are the possible advantages and disadvantages of this experience of childhood?

Feedback

You might think that there are no advantages for children living in single-parent families. It may appear to be a less than ideal situation! You might have this view because

⇨

of the general impression in our society that children's growth and development is enhanced by the nuclear family. It is, however, important to make sure that you do not overgeneralize and think that 'all nuclear families are ideal' and 'all single-parent families are not ideal'. Children can be highly perceptive. In other words, they 'sense' when they are loved and when they are not loved. If the children live in a nuclear family and the parents are constantly 'fighting', this can result in emotional difficulties for the children. They may feel unloved and this might have an adverse impact on their growth and development. In this situation it might actually be better for the children to be in a single-parent environment.

The increase of UK single-parent families

It is interesting to consider why there has been an increase in the number of children living in single-parent families in the United Kingdom. Haralambos and Holborn (1995, p.349) argue that the rise in single-parent families is closely related to the increase in the number of parents being divorced. From 1971 to 1991, the proportion of single lone mothers who were divorced rose from 21 per cent to 43 per cent. Haralambos and Holborn (1995, p.349) also cite that there was a rise in the percentage of single lone mothers. From 1971 to 1991 the figure changed from 16 per cent to 34 per cent. This suggests that the United Kingdom has become more accepting of diverse family forms. This point is made by David Morgan (1986) who argues that expectations of marriage have changed. Morgan also thinks that women have more opportunity to develop an independent life that does not depend on marriage or long-term cohabitation.

Haralambos and Holborn (1995, p.350) suggest that another important factor to take into consideration is the decline in stigma that is attached to single parenthood. This is reflected in the way that phrases such as 'illegitimate children' and 'unmarried mothers' are less likely to be used today because of their negative implications. This appears to suggest that the ways that many people think and talk about family life have changed quite considerably in recent years.

How this change in attitude towards families impacts upon the psychosocial welfare of children is a controversial and interesting question. Haralambos and Holborn (1995, p.351) cite the work of McLanahan and Booth to propose that children may be harmed by single parenthood. The argument runs that children in single-parent families have lower earnings and experience more poverty as adults. This research identified that children of 'mother-only' families are more likely to become lone parents themselves and that they are more likely to become 'delinquent' and engage in drug abuse.

Haralambos and Holborn (1995, p.351) challenge the assumption that children who are brought up by one parent are 'worse off' than children who are raised in a nuclear family environment. The work of Cashmere (1985) is applied to argue that it is often preferable for children to live with one 'loving' parent as opposed to being with 'one caring and one uncaring parent'. It would appear that as with any experience of childhood there are variations according to the individuals concerned. There are some children who appear to cope more effectively with their circumstances than other children. In order to ensure best practice, it is important to emphasize that the experience of childhood is not always perfect in one particular family type.

Case study

The Johnson family are one of the United Kingdom's many single-parent families. Three children aged eight, six and four live with their unemployed mother. The family members rely on state benefits for the majority of their income. The family's circumstances have had a significant impact on the children's development. There is never much money for the family to spend, so this means that the food that is available is not of good quality. Ms Johnson finds it very hard to support the children's learning as she never has enough money to buy the books and other learning materials that are required to stimulate the children's intellectual development. The children realize that their circumstances are different from other families around them. All of the children feel emotionally insecure. The children never have the latest technological devices that all the other children appear to want to play with and they usually have to make their own entertainment.

Reflective Activity 1.10

How will the Johnson children's physical, intellectual, emotional and social development be influenced by their circumstances?

Feedback

Although the children in the case study may get on well with each other, their development is likely to be influenced by their circumstances. If the family budget is

⇨

'limited', this is likely to mean that the children won't have a particularly good diet. This will influence the children's physical well-being. The case study also suggests that the family are unable to support the children's intellectual development as they do not have enough money to buy the learning materials that will reinforce the school's curriculum activities. The emotional insecurity and social isolation are also linked to their financial circumstances. The Johnson family may have a less positive experience of family life compared to other children in different circumstances.

The importance of ethnicity

Haralambos and Holborn (1995, p.351) draw attention to the importance of ethnicity in contributing to UK family diversity. The main ethnic groups who have immigrated into the United Kingdom have tended to adapt their ideas of family life to UK circumstances. Haralambos and Holborn (1995, p.351) go on to argue that the acceptance of cultural diversity within the United Kingdom has meant that family diversity is possible. It can also be argued that this in turn influences childhood experiences of family life.

The Social Trends (2009) statistics reveal differences in family type between different cultural groups. More than 50 per cent of black children live in single-parent families. This contrasts with Asian children as over 80 per cent of UK Indian dependent children live with married parents. This appears to suggest that the importance of marriage varies with cultural beliefs. This also appears to contribute to a different experience of childhood in the United Kingdom.

Haralambos and Holborn (1995, p.353) refer to the work of Roger Ballard to reveal how changing cultural circumstances influence family life. Ballard (1990) has popularized how South Asian family life can change as a result of emigration to the United Kingdom. Whereas South Asian families are traditionally based around a man, his sons, and grandsons, migration to the United Kingdom can lead to an increasingly important economic role for women. This is in turn likely to impact upon the experiences of childhood as women become more associated with wage labour. Ballard suggests that families are more likely to be split into smaller domestic groupings as a result of these changing economic circumstances alongside the United Kingdom cultural expectation that 'extended families' are not the usual family type.

Case study

Dwight is seven. His ethnic background is Afro-Caribbean and he lives with his mother and two older brothers. Dwight has never known his father. The only male role models that Dwight has ever been close to are his two older brothers. Dwight has become emotionally close to his oldest brother and he has been visibly affected by his brother's recent arrest for possessing cannabis and belonging to a violent gang. Dwight's mother and brothers cannot accept that possessing cannabis and being in a gang can be against the law as it is accepted as a cultural norm within the wider local community. Dwight 'hero worships' his older brother, and at a recent community liaison event he refused to speak to the local police representatives. Dwight's mother is anxious about what will happen to him in the future. She thinks that his childhood days should be the happiest of his life. It saddens her to think that at the age of seven he is already aware of community tensions.

Reflective Activity 1.11

How is Dwight's cultural background influencing his experience of childhood?

Feedback

You may think that too many UK children appear to 'grow-up' too quickly and lose their childhood at an early age. In the above case study, Dwight's mother is anxious that the challenges of the modern world are already having a negative impact on Dwight's experience of childhood. You could argue that childhood experiences should not be influenced negatively by 'differing cultural beliefs'. On the other hand, you might also argue that unless all cultural groups follow the same legal system, social tensions and potential anarchy may result. In the case study, it appears that Dwight's cultural background is at odds with UK law. His experience of childhood is more influenced by his cultural background than by his identity as a UK citizen. This appears to be at the centre of the tensions that the family are experiencing.

Family breakdown

It can be argued that 'family breakdown' is becoming more apparent within UK society. Haralambos and Holborn (1995, p.370) cite the decline in the popularity of marriage alongside the increasing occurrence of marital breakdown as evidence that the United Kingdom is witnessing an increased amount of family breakdown. It can also be argued that despite these two social trends, most people in the United Kingdom still live in families, so it is important not to overemphasize the importance of family breakdown.

The argument that there are 'threats to marriage' in the United Kingdom has been presented for a number of years. Robert Chester (1985) drew attention to the decline in marriage rates among young adults in Western countries such as Sweden, Denmark, the United Kingdom, Germany and the USA. The statistics supporting this change in trends reveal that in 1971, one in eleven teenage women was married. By 1981 this had fallen to one in twenty-four. Alongside this statistic, Haralambos and Holborn (1995, p.370) cite that between 1981 and 1990, the marriage rate in the United Kingdom for all age groups fell from 7.1 per year per thousand of all the eligible population, to 6.8.

UK statistical data does appear to show that family trends have changed over times. The number of single-parents with dependent children rose from 1.6 million in 1997 to 2 million in 2012 (Social Trends (2012)). These changing family trends are referred to by Joan Chandler (1991) in her research into UK 'cohabitation' or 'living together'. Chandler argues that the social convention to 'marry first and then have children' has lessened within the United Kingdom. This appears to be an important factor influencing UK family life. This will in turn have a significant impact on UK children's experience of childhood.

Reflective Activity 1.12

A number of religions in the United Kingdom regard marriage as a 'sacrament'. If lots of UK couples do not accept this interpretation of marriage, how might this affect their children's experience of childhood?

Feedback

It can be argued that as with many forms of social life, differing interpretations of 'right and wrong' have differing 'advantages and disadvantages'. To view marriage as a 'sacrament' and having a 'spiritual' quality can be a great advantage if this means that a couple love each other and consider their children to be a 'gift' or a 'blessing'. The advantage of this view can be seen in many UK families who appear to have a strong belief in the importance of marriage as a 'sacred sacrament'. This belief can appear to inform their loyalty and commitment to the family. It can also be argued that as long as this view of family life does not become intolerant of others who do not share the same belief, it will make a positive contribution to UK social life.

> **Practical task**
>
> When you are next on the internet, visit the United Kingdom Social Trends website. Try to find out more information about UK family trends affecting the experience of childhood from the Social Trends statistical data.

Marital breakdown

Haralambos and Holborn (1995, p.370) argue that there are three main categories of marital breakdown. These are listed as 'divorce'; 'separation'; and 'empty-shell marriage'. Divorce can be defined as being 'legal separation' whereas 'separation' differs from divorce because there are not the same legal implications. 'Empty-shell marriage' is a term that is used to describe couples who are legally married but their marriage exists in name only.

The UK Social Trends statistics reveal that there has been a steady rise in divorce rates. The number of divorces occurring in Britain doubled between 1958 and 1969. Social Trends (2006) reveals that in 2004, the number of UK divorces was 167,100. This represents a fourth successive yearly rise.

This UK divorce rate is very high compared to other European countries. Haralambos and Holborn (1995, p.372) record that only Denmark had a higher rate in 1990. Although it is relatively easy to quantify the number of divorces, it is more difficult to identify the number of instances of 'separation' and 'empty-shell marriages'. Haralambos and Holborn (1995, p.372) propose that whereas the instance of UK separation has probably increased, the extent of empty-shell marriage has lessened. It can be proposed that this is because of the changing attitude to relationships within the United Kingdom. This echoes Ingleby and Hunt's (2008) argument that the 'social discourse' or ways of talking about relationships have changed over time within the United Kingdom. An emphasis is now placed upon the rights of the individual as opposed to emphasizing the importance of 'society' and 'institutions'.

Nicky Hart (1976) explains marital breakdown by considering the 'value' that is given to marriage, the level of 'conflict' that exists between spouses and the degree of possibility of 'escaping' from marriage. If marriage is not highly valued, if conflict levels are high within the marriage and if it is easy to 'escape' from marital ties, there is a greater possibility of the marriage 'failing'. All three factors do appear to have become a 'norm' within UK family life in general.

Divorce legislation

The changing attitude to divorce within the United Kingdom has been institutionalized by a number of changes in the law. These legal changes have made it easier to obtain a divorce settlement. Haralambos and Holborn (1995, p.374) acknowledge that before 1857, a private act of parliament was required to obtain a divorce. This procedure was not possible for the majority of the population because it was very expensive.

Since 1857, divorce costs have fallen and the grounds for divorce have been widened. The 1971 Divorce Reform Act defined the grounds for divorce as 'the irretrievable breakdown of the marriage'. This has made divorce easier and helps to explain why there has been such a dramatic rise in the number of divorces in the United Kingdom since 1971.

Additional divorce legislation was also introduced at the end of 1984. This legislation reduced the period that a couple needed to be married before they could petition for divorce from three years to one. The legislation also made the 'behaviour of the married partners' the key influencing factor in deciding marriage settlements. This meant that if the behaviour of one partner was the key factor leading to the divorce, the other partner's 'liability' would be reduced in the subsequent divorce settlement.

Reflective Activity 1.13

Do you think that divorce rates will continue to rise in the United Kingdom? How do you think this will influence children's experiences of childhood?

Feedback

If the Social Trends statistics are to be believed, then it would appear to suggest that the number of divorces will continue to rise. Of course, this might not mean that marriage is less popular. It might mean that there is more marriage if divorced people re-marry. The Social Trends statistics appear to support this argument. They reveal that the figure of 286,100 marriages in 2001 rose to 308,600 in 2003. Despite this statistic, it appears to be the case that divorce is a pertinent UK social trend. In 2010, 42 per cent of all marriages ended in divorce. (although this figure was less than the 45 per cent of marriages that ended in divorce in 2005). This will have an impact on children's experience of childhood within the United Kingdom. We have already mentioned that within the United Kingdom, concern has been expressed about children 'growing up too soon'. Perhaps this happens because of the lack of stability within many UK families? This might result in the experience of childhood becoming 'negative', resulting in a wish to 'move on' to the adult world. If this is true, it once again provides another different experience of childhood.

Summary of key points

In this chapter we began by explaining that some sociological theories focus on the importance of wider society. In contrast, other sociological theories emphasize the importance of individuals. We have also seen that there is not one universal type of family. The family differs according to time and space. In other words, through history and through culture there are differing family types. Becoming aware of the changing nature of the family allows you to become more aware of individual needs. This in turn connects your professional work to 'best practice' when you are working with children and families. The chapter has also revealed how UK families have been influenced by cultural trends. It would appear that one of the most important factors influencing UK families is the experience of 'family breakdown'. All of these factors have a tremendous influence on children's experience of childhood. It can be argued that one of the most fascinating aspects of applying social science to early years is witnessing the variety of children's experiences within the known world. Children appear to engage with the world around them and interpret these experiences in a unique way. The essence of studying children appears to rest in this diversity of experience. To be aware of this characteristic appears to be the best way of applying social science to early years.

Self-assessment questions

Question 1
Is the 'nuclear family' a universal family type?

Question 2
What are two important factors that appear to influence family form?

Question 3
What is one of the key factors influencing UK children's experience of childhood today?

Moving on

This chapter has introduced you to the idea of how family type influences childhood experiences. You might want to think of developing some research ideas within this area of study in order to contribute to your continuing professional development.

Further reading

Haralambos, M. and Holborn, M. (2008), *Sociology: Themes and Perspectives*. London: Collins.

A useful textbook in terms of clarity of content and analysis but the material is not always directly related to early years contexts.

Yeo, A. and Lovell, T. (2003), *Sociology for Childhood Studies*. London: Hodder & Stoughton.

An excellent textbook that is written in an accessible way and makes clear links in identifying how the family influences children's experiences of childhood.

Raising Awareness of the Developing Child and Best Practice

2

Learning outcomes

After reading this chapter you should be able to:

- identify how awareness of the physical, intellectual, emotional and social development of children helps us to develop best practice when we are working with children and families;
- analyse the benefits of raised awareness of the physical, intellectual, emotional and social development of children when we are working with children and families;
- critically appraise the contribution made by social science to our understanding of children's physical, intellectual emotional and social development;
- recognize the importance of effective communication when we are working with children and families.

Introduction

Working with children and families can never be a static experience! Children and families change all the time. This chapter explores the implications of the developing child for children's services. The chapter explores the contribution that social science makes in understanding the physical, intellectual, emotional and social development of children. The first area of child development that is explored considers research into the effects of social problems (for example, poverty, poor diet and domestic abuse) on children and families. The chapter then applies the work of Piaget, Vygotsky and Gardner in order to outline how differing approaches to pedagogy inform our understanding of children's intellectual development. In developing the point that it is important to become aware of children's emotional development, the person-centred philosophy of Carl Rogers is amplified in order to help us to understand why anxiety occurs in children. If we are to embrace best practice, it is important to ensure that anxiety does not affect children's emotional development adversely. In order to become more aware of the importance of children's emotional development, it is helpful to consider the theory of transactional analysis that is outlined by Eric Berne. Transactional analysis can enable us to ensure that children's social development occurs as assertively as possible. The chapter considers how our understanding of child development has emerged over time. In order to ensure best practice, it is vital to maximize opportunities for children to develop as effectively as possible. The content of the chapter also considers how our professional practice can be enhanced through becoming aware of the importance of effective communication with children and families. This helps us to appreciate the interplay between a number of key factors that contribute to child development, our professional practice. Our subsequent awareness of best practice is thus enhanced.

Understanding child development

Reflective Activity 2.1

What is child development?

Feedback

The obvious answer to this question is that 'child development' is understood as being how children grow and change over time. A helpful way of understanding the range of factors that influence child development is to consider how children grow and develop physically, intellectually, emotionally and socially. This allows us to focus on key parts of child development by considering research and theory from within social science subjects including sociology, psychology and social policy. A holistic understanding of child development is then possible and this enables us to develop our awareness of best professional practice.

The physical development of children

From birth onwards, children change physically. Psychologists including Piaget and Vygotsky have drawn attention to the link between children's physical development and their subsequent changes in thought processes. Although it is important to make sure that we acknowledge the connections between the various elements of child development (physical, intellectual, emotional and social), it is helpful to emphasize the importance of children's physical development in its own right. Moreover, there are a number of social problems (for example, poverty, poor diet and domestic violence) that have consequences for intellectual, emotional and social development but have particular effects on children's physical development.

The consequences of poverty for children's physical growth and development

Reflective Activity 2.2

What is poverty?

Feedback

There are three types of poverty that are written about within social science research. There is what is referred to as 'absolute poverty'. If someone is living in absolute poverty, there is the likelihood that they will die as a result of their poor circumstances. 'Relative poverty' is a type of poverty that can only be understood in relation to others. A person who is poor in the United Kingdom today may be considered as being 'rich' if they were placed in another cultural context experiencing absolute poverty. 'Subjective poverty' is a personal understanding that the individual is living in a state of poverty. This personal definition of poverty may not be shared by others.

Poverty is one of the major social problems for children and families that has been commented on within the United Kingdom. In exemplifying this argument, the paintings of the artist Augustus Mulready draw attention to the extent of poverty within nineteenth-century London. The urban society depicted by Mulready was full of contradictions, with its affluent minority being dwarfed by an enormous underclass of children and families living in absolute poverty. At this time in the United Kingdom, little was done to help poor children and families by the state. In the nineteenth century, there was no such thing as the NHS or state social work. Children and families relied in general on family and friends and the work of the voluntary sector. It was at this time that many of the voluntary organizations like Barnado's came into being.

The poverty that was experienced by children and families in the nineteenth century was so absolute that it led to a literal loss due to death on a vast scale. Horn (1997) outlines that in London alone in 1848 there were in the region of 'more than thirty thousand deserted children roaming the metropolis'. Horn (1997) goes on to acknowledge that these children experienced such severe levels of poverty that it led to concerns that the entire fabric of society would be destroyed!

The absolute poverty experienced by these children is not unfamiliar to us today. There are countries in the developing world (for example, in Sudan) that are also experiencing absolute poverty. Moreover, there are still many children experiencing poverty in the United Kingdom today. According to Barnado's, in 2014, there are 3.5 million children living in poverty in the United Kingdom (about one-third of all children). 1.6 million of these children are defined as living in severe poverty. Barnado's has identified that this experience of poverty produces significant health consequences for children. Children aged three, who live in households earning less than £10,000, are 2.5 times more likely to suffer chronic illness than those living in households with incomes above £52,000. Moreover, infant mortality is 10 per cent higher for children living in households earning less than £10,000. Barnado's has identified that families living in poverty can have as little as £12 per day per person to live on. 1.6 million children are identified as living in homes that are too cold, with this experience of poverty inevitably having consequences for the physical health and well-being of children.

Reflective Activity 2.3

What are the physical effects of poverty on children?

Feedback

The worst form of poverty is absolute poverty. In this type of poverty, there is the likelihood that the child will die as a result of poverty. There is not enough food for the child to eat. Their physical development is not enabled because they lack all that is essential for their growth and development. Children are also more vulnerable to illnesses if they are living in poverty. Their immunity levels are likely to be lower, so they are less likely to be able to resist illnesses. All aspects of growth and development are likely to be affected adversely.

Reflective Activity 2.4

How can practitioners working in early years help children who are experiencing poverty?

Feedback

We have seen that poverty has been an issue affecting children and families in the United Kingdom for centuries. We may not have the experience of absolute poverty in the United Kingdom today, but the data from Barnado's outlines that poverty is still a significant problem affecting children and families today. A difficulty with statements such as '3.5 million children live in poverty' is that poverty is experienced differently according to context. The experience of poverty may have increased in the north-east of England whereas in other areas of the country, poverty is less of an issue. To help children who are experiencing poverty, many early years settings provide children with free meals, warm clothes and liaise with other agencies in social services. It is important for practitioners to provide the actual physical help and support for these children in order to enable them to deal with their experience of poverty.

Poor diet and its consequences for children's physical development

Reflective Activity 2.5

What is a poor diet?

Feedback

It is important to ensure that a 'poor diet' is not equated with 'having little to eat'. You do not need to be hungry to experience a poor diet (although a 'poor diet' and 'having little to eat' may be regarded by some as being the same thing). Poor diet is more to do with having an imbalance of nutrients. There is not enough fruit, vegetables, fat and carbohydrates to provide a balanced diet. Nutrition intake is confined to a few sources of food.

Poor diet is another social problem that has a significant impact on children's physical growth and development. Like poverty, it is a social problem that has been present in the United Kingdom for a number of years. Like poverty too, the emphasis placed by the media tends to be more on the consequences of poor diet for children and families in the developing world. As we shall see, poor diet has significant consequences for children and families in the United Kingdom today.

In 2014, the Health & Social Care Information Centre provided the following summary of how poor diet is producing physical consequences for UK children and families. The proportion of the population with a 'normal' Body Mass Index decreased during 1993–2012 from 41 per cent to 32 per cent in men and from 49.5 per cent to 40.6 per cent among women. There was a significant increase in the proportion of the population who were identified as being 'obese' between 1993 and 2012 (from 13.2 per cent to 24.4 per cent of men and from 16.4 per cent to 25.1 per cent of women). A contributory factor to these statistics appears to be the levels of inactivity in men and women. Twenty-six per cent of women and 19 per cent of men were classed as being inactive. A further mitigating factor is that overall purchases of fresh fruit and vegetables were reduced between 2009 and 2012. These statistics outline that 'poor diet' is a significant social problem in the United Kingdom. The saying 'you are what you eat' explains why there is so much concern with unhealthy diets in children in the United Kingdom. If children eat diets that are unhealthy, they are likely to be unhealthy too! There is what is referred to as a 'ticking time bomb' of health issues that are consequences of these inappropriate and unhealthy diets.

Reflective Activity 2.6

What are the physical effects of poor diet on children?

Feedback

Poor diets in children lead to physical health problems. A child can only grow and develop if they are receiving adequate nutrition. If their diet is 'poor', they will not be able to grow and develop effectively. Moreover, a poor diet is likely to result in a weakened immune system. Hirst and Woolley (1982) outline that many of the 'big killers' in nineteenth-century UK society (for example, pneumonia and tuberculosis) were linked fundamentally to diet. In today's society, too much fat can lead to eventual problems such as heart disease and a diet that is lacking fruit and vegetables can increase the chances of developing cancer in later life.

> ### Reflective Activity 2.7
>
> How can early years practitioners help children who are experiencing poor diets?
>
> #### Feedback
>
> There are examples of nursery settings and schools that provide children with a healthy meal as they are within the setting. As well as the literal provision of a healthy diet, it is also possible to educate the children about what makes a healthy diet and how diet has a fundamental link to future good health.

Domestic violence and its consequences for children's growth and development

What is domestic violence?

Domestic violence is violence in the home. It is often associated with a man being violent towards his 'wife' and/or children. Like poverty, domestic violence has a long history in the United Kingdom. It is a major problem within society.

Domestic violence is not usually associated with women being physically violent towards men and the statistics in the United Kingdom about domestic violence support this point. The NSPCC (2014) outline that in a study of 139 serious case reviews in England from 2009 to 2011, 63 per cent had domestic abuse as a factor. Twelve per cent of children aged under one year had experienced some form of domestic abuse, with males being the perpetrators in 94 per cent of cases where one parent had physically abused another. Moreover, domestic abuse accounts for 14 per cent of all violent crime. These figures are exacerbated by the statistic that in the United Kingdom between 1994 and 2004, twenty-nine children in thirteen families were killed as a consequence of domestic violence. Ten of these children were killed in the last two years. The total cost of domestic violence to the state amounts to £3.8 billion each year (the criminal justice system, health and social care costs). It is estimated that if we factor in the human and emotional costs, this amounts to a figure in the region of £10 billion each year.

Reflective Activity 2.8

What are the physical effects of domestic violence on children?

Feedback

In his powerful novel *Sons and Lovers*, D.H. Lawrence (1992) draws attention to the physical effects of domestic abuse on the family. The novel is about a family who live in a mining community. The father of the family is especially violent after drinking alcohol. Lawrence writes about the physical violence inflicted on the family members. He writes about a contrasting world where there is peace and harmony in the day and violence and discord at night. The family's world becomes a place of terror as a consequence of domestic violence. The sheer physical terror experienced by the children is described as impacting on all aspects of their physical development. The children are so terrified that they are unable to sleep at night and lie in their beds listening to the wind shrieking through the trees. Their world is explained as being what we might expect to be the opposite of a happy family life.

Reflective Activity 2.9

How can early years practitioners help children who are experiencing domestic violence?

Feedback

Staff in early years settings are likely to receive training that will help them to identify whether children show the physical effects of domestic violence. If a child has a series of severe and repeated injuries, this may be a sign that they are a victim of domestic violence. The early years setting may then liaise with social services in order to encourage further intervention so that the child is removed from the abusive home. Domestic violence may lead to the children lacking confidence and performing poorly in school. There may be individual interventions to help these children, with specialist help and support for their subsequent education.

The intellectual development of children

There are a number of theorists and theories within social science associated with the intellectual development of children. Becoming aware of these theorists and their associated theories helps us when we are working with children and families, especially if we are educating children. This section of the chapter considers the developmental ideas of Jean Piaget and Lev Vygotsky alongside the work of Howard Gardner. These psychologists have formulated a powerful set of ideas about the intellectual development of children. In becoming aware of their theories, our ability to work effectively with children and families is enhanced. This in turn influences our employability potential.

The work of Piaget

The Swiss psychologist Jean Piaget has made a significant contribution to understanding the intellectual development of children. Piaget draws attention to the ways that children's minds develop over time. Cognitive ability depends upon the age and experience of the child. Moreover, the child's cognitive abilities are influenced by the sorts of experiences that they have as they are growing and developing. These ideas are especially useful if we are working with children in a pedagogical capacity.

Piaget argues that the first component of a child's cognitive development is referred to as the 'sensorimotor' stage. Piaget claims that this occurs between the ages of zero and two years. At this stage of the child's life, they are in possession of what Piaget refers to as 'basic or instinctive thoughts'. These thoughts are described by Piaget as 'schema' or 'schemata'. There is a 'feeding schema', a 'crying schema' and a 'grasping schema'. As the infant interacts with its environment, these cognitive abilities change and develop accordingly. As the child moves beyond the age of two years, it enters what Piaget describes as a 'preoperational stage' of cognition. As the child learns to speak, so it learns to interact with the environment in a more complicated, 'more human' way. The child's thinking processes become more than 'instinctive', 'animal-like' thoughts. The beginnings of a distinctive human way of thinking start to appear. By the age of seven years, children are capable of solving intellectual problems through what Piaget refers to as 'concrete operations'. At this stage of development, the child can solve 'complex' problems (for example, mathematical problems) as long as the props (or 'concrete objects') are at hand. In working out the sum '7 + 2', it helps the child if it has 7 discrete objects to add to 2 discrete objects. Piaget claims that it is only after the age of eleven that children are able to complete complex problems 'in their heads'.

Reflective Activity 2.10

How can the work of Piaget be used to enhance employability and professional practice?

Feedback

Piaget's views are very useful when we are working in learning and teaching contexts with children and families. His theory of the mind is helpful if we are working with children aged 2–7 years as an emphasis is placed on the importance of enabling practical learning activities with children. There is little to be gained from lecturing these children! They are much more likely to learn if the pedagogy we use with them is as practical as possible. Becoming aware of these ideas is thus likely to enable us to become more effective at teaching and more employable.

The developmental theory of Lev Vygotsky

The Russian psychologist Lev Vygotsky has popularized the importance of 'social learning'. Vygotsky considers that all of us have a particular amount of potential within us to learn. The potential to learn is referred to as being our 'zone of proximal development' (or ZPD). Vygotsky argues that the purpose of the education system is to enable us to reach this level of potential or ability. His work draws attention to the importance of ensuring that learning potential is developed through positive social interaction with other learners. The learners are visualized as forming a social 'scaffold' to support the individual learner in order to enable the realization of potential. For this to happen, it is essential to ensure that those children in the 'learning scaffold' are able to nurture social development.

Reflective Activity 2.11

How can the work of Vygotsky be used to enhance employability and professional practice?

Feedback

Vygotsky's work draws attention to the importance of ensuring that social learning occurs. Learning does not happen in isolation. Vygotsky argues that the learning process is fundamentally linked to interaction with others. Whereas Piaget may be associated with focusing on each individual learner, Vygotsky draws attention to the importance of others in the learning process. A 'scaffold' of learners is placed round the individual in order to develop potential. If we are working in early years we need to ensure that learning activities become 'social' with children working together in small groups. These small groups of learners form a scaffold that can help the child to realize its potential. Many of the early years settings include clusters of children gathered together according to ability. The purpose of gathering these learners together is to ensure that learning is fundamentally social. In becoming aware of the importance of social learning, our professional practice is improved and our employability is enhanced.

The work of Howard Gardner

Alcock et al. (2000, p. 321) argue that recent governments have adopted a partnership approach to UK society by emphasizing the importance of 'values of community, responsibility and social solidarity'. A consequence of this approach within education in early years is to regard 'educators' and 'those being educated' as 'working together'. This has affected those who would have previously been unable to adjust to the demands of the educational system, for example, children with 'challenging behaviour' and children with 'special educational needs'. As opposed to excluding children who cannot meet the demands of the education system, another approach is needed. This requires the education system to adapt to the needs of children who have previously been excluded.

The impact of this approach is the implementation of learning strategies that are based on the ideas of Howard Gardner (1984, 1993 and 2000). Gardner proposes that there are eight forms of intelligence. These forms of intelligence are described by Gardner as being 'visual spatial', 'linguistic', 'logical mathematical', 'musical', 'bodily kinaesthetic', 'interpersonal', 'intrapersonal' and 'naturalistic' intelligence. Supporters of Gardner's ideas argue that the traditional educational system is based on 'linguistic' and 'logical mathematical' intelligence. The argument runs that the educational system can become more inclusive if it acknowledges other categories of intelligence and in turn incorporates activities to develop these 'other' skills and abilities. This has led to the introduction of 'learning inventories' that attempt to identify the preferred learning style of groups of learners.

Strengths and weaknesses of multiple intelligences

The attention that has been given to multiple intelligences can be seen as being positive if it leads to a more innovative curriculum for early years. This curriculum innovation can be used to enhance our awareness of learning and teaching in early years and in turn improve our employability skills. Coffield et al.'s (2004) research into learning styles does acknowledge that there are potential benefits in establishing learning inventories. This allows the possibility of tailoring teaching and learning in order to meet the needs of the learners. As opposed to making the curriculum an aspect of education that is 'followed by the learners', a raised awareness of learning styles can allow for more innovative teaching and learning activities. If the group's learning preference is predominantly 'visual spatial', this can be used to justify 'visual spatial' learning activities. Coffield et al.'s (2004) research also gives a critique of learning styles. It is possible to ask: 'why are there eight types of intelligence?' 'why not nine or ten or more?' Another critique of the implementation of learning inventories is that it adds on another layer of bureaucracy to the heavily bureaucratic teaching profession. This may mean that being aware of learning styles becomes more of an aspect of 'audit' to impress education inspectors than an innovative part of the educational curriculum.

Reflective Activity 2.12

Give a critical appraisal of recent governments' acceptance of 'multiple intelligences'.

Feedback

Coffield et al.'s (2004) research appears to question the validity of the concept of 'multiple intelligences'. This argument can be developed to question the nature of the educational policy-making. Critics including Lucas (2007) argue that too much education is 'standards driven'. In other words, the educational process is not being fully acknowledged. The literal meaning of the word 'education' implies that the individual ought to be enabled to see the world differently. This is less likely to happen if education is 'standards driven'. If multiple intelligences are applied to education to impress inspectors, this will not mean that they become an integral part of learning. They are instead akin to bureaucratic tasks that are standards-driven as opposed to being designed to educate individuals in the truest sense of the term. Coffield et al. (2004) argue for a return to the notion of 'Platonic kings' – in other words, for educationalists who are experts in practice and in turn able to shape educational policies. Perhaps this idea should be at the centre of future early years educational policies?

Reflective Activity 2.13

How can the work of Piaget, Vygotsky and Gardner be combined together to become beneficial for practitioners in early years?

Feedback

If we apply the principles of holistic practice when we are working with children and families, we are more likely to combine ideas in our professional practice. By combining the theories of Piaget, Vygotsky and Gardner we are able to apply a strong theoretical framework to our learning and teaching activities. As noted previously, the advantage of applying Piaget's work is that we have a theoretical understanding of how and why children's cognitive processes develop and change over time. Piaget's stages of cognitive development draw attention to the different cognitive processes within children. The early years (up to age eight) are a time when children learn in a practical way. They need 'props' or physical objects that help them to learn. Lots of current initiatives in early years (for example, forest schools) are based on practical learning as opposed to didactic teaching. It is Piaget who draws attention to this practical learning.

The work of Vygotsky helps us to realize the importance of social learning. Children cannot fulfil their academic potential if they are working in isolation. They ought to have other learners working alongside them so that they are able to reach their full academic potential. These other learners create the social circumstances that are necessary for the individual child to fulfil its potential. If we are responsible for arranging teaching and learning activities, it becomes essential for us to ensure that there is a social component to learning. This may take the form of a learning activity that enables others to work together in a small group. By adopting this approach to learning and teaching activities we thus show that we are aware of the importance of ensuring that there is a 'scaffold' of learners helping the child to realize its cognitive development.

As well as demonstrating awareness of the importance of stages of cognitive development and social learning, it is also important to consider the ideas of Howard Gardner if our teaching in early years is to be characterized by best practice. Not all children enjoy 'linguistic' and 'logical mathematical' tasks, yet so much of the academic curriculum is based on these learning activities. There are children with tremendous abilities at art and music. Gardner argues that it is just as important to include this learning within the formal curriculum. Learning the craft of teaching requires us to be flexible in our understanding of pedagogy. We need to reflect on what has worked well alongside considering what needs to change if our teaching is to improve in the future. By applying the ideas of Piaget, Vygotsky and Gardner we are in turn able to ensure that our teaching in early years is informed by theories about learning and teaching in this area. This can help us to meet the intellectual needs of children in a powerful and profound way. Moreover, this leads to our pedagogy becoming informed by reflecting on how children learn and which teaching techniques are going to get the most out of our learners.

The emotional development of children

For children's growth and development to be effective, it is important that there is consideration of all aspects of their development. Critics of the academic curriculum in England (for example, Urban (2008)) draw attention to the 'uncertainty' that can be present within us when we are working with children and families. These feelings of uncertainty may be present if we are working with children who are studying a curriculum that is dominated by a few core subjects (for example, English, science and maths). So much emphasis may be placed on these core subjects that it becomes difficult to focus on the emotional aspects of the child's development. To help raise our awareness of 'best practice' (and to increase our prospects of employability), it is important to recognize how theorists from social science can contribute to informing our understanding of how to develop children's emotional security effectively. A social scientist who is helpful regarding this aspect of child development is Carl Rogers. A strength of Rogers' work is that it outlines why, when and how children are likely to become anxious. It can be argued that anxiety is a mitigating factor affecting children's emotional development. In applying the work of Carl Rogers to our professional practice, we are more likely to have an increased awareness of how children's emotional development can be enhanced.

The developmental theory of Carl Rogers

Carl Rogers is associated with humanism. Within humanism an emphasis is placed upon the importance of individuals. The environment and the mind are not the focus of this particular school of thought. Attention is drawn to studying how the individual shapes his/her social world. A particularly useful aspect of Rogers' work is his explanation of what causes anxiety. As opposed to exploring the complex neurological reasons why individuals are anxious, Rogers' work offers a simple explanation for why some individuals become anxious. Rogers argues that anxiety is a product of what he refers to as a 'would-should dilemma'. In other words, the individual wants to do something but they are not able to achieve this wish. All sorts of simple examples can be used to reveal what the 'would-should' dilemma is. A child wants to play with a particular toy, but other children refuse to allow the child to play with the toy. This promotes anxiety in the child and leads to a 'would-should dilemma'. Rogers claims that when children experience anxiety, they are suffering from a 'would-should' dilemma. The more of these dilemmas that are being faced by the child, the more anxiety and tension is within the child. This will, in turn, have consequences for the emotional security of the child. The argument runs that children who are extremely anxious are less likely to be able to develop emotional security. Moreover, there is the possibility of children experiencing a series of 'would-should' dilemmas. If a child is unable to do what it would like to do frequently in multiple areas, this will increase the child's levels of anxiety and impact upon the child's emotional development.

Reflective Activity 2.14

Is anxiety a significant factor that affects children in the United Kingdom and mitigates against their emotional development?

Feedback

The Mental Health Foundation has revealed how extensive a problem anxiety is in children and young people in the United Kingdom. The statistics outline that one in four people in the United Kingdom will develop some sort of mental health problem. Moreover, anxiety is considered to be one of the most common mental disorders in England, with 10 per cent of children identified as having a mental health problem. It is claimed that rates of mental health problems in children increase into adolescence, with disorders affecting 10.4 per cent of boys aged 5–10 rising to 12.8 per cent of boys aged 11–15 and 5.9 per cent of girls aged 5–10 rising to 9.65 per cent of girls aged 11–15.

What are the emotional effects of anxiety on children?

If children are to develop, it is important that they feel emotionally secure. In order to have the confidence to communicate effectively with others, it is important to be emotionally secure. If a child is not in possession of this sense of security, they are unlikely to be able to connect with others socially. Their anxiety is likely to result in feelings of low self-esteem. If this negative self-worth is being experienced by children, they are in turn unlikely to become confident enough to develop the necessary emotional security that will enable their growth and development.

Reflective Activity 2.15

What can early years workers do to help children to develop emotionally?

Feedback

If we apply the ideas of Carl Rogers, it is important to reflect on how we can make the children we work with as emotionally secure as possible. One way we can do this is by being consistent. Children appear to appreciate a secure environment that provides their daily lives with structure. We might consider ensuring that the daily routine within the early years setting is structured in such a way that it provides security for the child's day. As opposed to asking 'what do you want to do today?', we establish a routine that is consistent. This is likely to help the children feel more confident and secure. The children are in turn able to develop in a positive way as a result of these feelings of emotional security. The timetable studied by the children can help them achieve feelings of security. A set curriculum that is a combination of a series of established academic subjects will be taught over similar days within the school year. This can help the children feel secure with the school week. The children are in school to learn. If they are able to learn well as a result of a clear and consistent timetable, this will help them to have the security that is required if they are to develop the necessary emotional security. Conversely, if the children find that they struggle with the academic curriculum, this can mean that they associate the school environment with negative feelings. This is in turn, more likely to make them have feelings of anxiety. Their emotional skills are thus less likely to develop as effectively as they should.

Reflective Activity 2.16

How are the ideas of Carl Rogers likely to help us improve our professional practice and thus improve our prospects of employability?

Feedback

When we are working with children and families it is easy to assume that it is most important to ensure that the children are 'kept busy' and 'occupied'. If we are working in a teaching capacity, it is also easy to become so involved with the curriculum that we lose sight of the emotional development of children. The advantage with Rogers is that he draws attention to the importance of a particular form of teaching with children. The emphasis is not placed on 'effective didactic delivery'. An emphasis is placed instead on ensuring that 'congruence' is established between the learners and the teacher. A 'congruent' teacher is a genuine teacher who is there for the learners and a genuinely good person. Rogers emphasizes aspects of learning and teaching that are to do with 'congruence' as opposed to focusing upon 'achievement' or 'a national curriculum'. Another phrase that is highlighted by Rogers is the idea that students ought to become 'architects of their own destiny'. Rogers' model of teaching is based on enabling others to become empowered. The teacher is encouraged to become a facilitator of learning as opposed to directing the learning process in a way that omits to take the views of the learners into consideration. Within social care, it is often claimed at anecdotal level that there are some staff who appear to make a connection with children who have behavioural and/or emotional disorders. This is often because they have the professional skills that enable the children to grow and develop. These staff may appear to be especially 'calm'. This can in turn help the children feel 'relaxed'. Their experience of the learning environment is subsequently less stressful. The children's emotional security is in turn enhanced. Much of this 'good practice' is based on the ideas of Carl Rogers. Within our professional relationships it is essential that we become 'enabling' of the development of the emotional security of the children we are working with. As opposed to placing too much emphasis on intellectual development it is essential to make sure that other aspects of child development are considered. If we become congruent professionals who are able to make this connection with the children we work with, this will in turn enhance our employability. Of course, it is essential to have the cognitive skills that are necessary to work effectively with children and families. The skills of effective communication and selflessness are, however, just as important if we are to work well with children and families and in turn enhance our skills of employability. As the statistics presented in this section of the chapter outline, there are significant numbers of children who are experiencing anxiety. In order to help these children to develop their emotional security, we can apply the ideas of Rogers and in turn help to ease as many 'would-should' dilemmas as we can.

The social development of children

If children are to become a next generation who are 'safe', it is important for them to develop social skills. It can be argued that the social skills of human beings are part of the defining characteristics that make us human beings! This section of the chapter explores how we can develop the social skills of children through applying the work of the Canadian psychologist Eric Berne. A benefit of his work is that an emphasis is placed upon encouraging the development of assertiveness within individuals. According to Berne, to be 'assertive' is to behave in a way that is appropriate and reasonable. If we become aware of developing an assertive and appropriate personality within children, we are in turn more likely to enable the development of children's social skills. This will be a further example of best practice and another way of ensuring that our employability is enhanced.

The work of Eric Berne

Transactional Analysis has been developed by the Canadian psychologist Eric Berne (1910–1970). It can be argued that transactional analysis (or 'TA') has made an influential and interesting contribution to understanding human communication. The advantage of Berne's theory is that it is accessible and it can be used to interpret the quality of communication occurring between individuals and groups. Berne's Transactional Analysis proposes that all individuals have three components to their personality. Berne uses the phrase 'ego states' to explain these components of personality. According to the theory there are 'parent', 'adult' and 'child' states. The 'parent state' represents authoritarian characteristics of personality. The 'adult state' represents appropriate interaction. The 'child state' represents interaction that is characterized by emotional impulses. Berne argues that all of these categories are present in adults and children. They govern our interpersonal communication.

The theory proposes that when people communicate, they do so according to 'parent', 'child' or 'adult' states. If an appropriate (or 'adult' question) is asked, for example: 'How do you feel today?', there are a number of possible responses. An appropriate adult response may be given such as: 'I feel fine!'; Berne would describe this transaction as 'adult to adult' appropriate interaction. The argument runs that if all of our transactions are characterized by appropriate 'adult to adult' interaction, our communication will be high quality and our emotional security will be enhanced.

Berne recognizes that many transactions between individuals and groups are not characterized by positive communication methods. There are what are referred to as 'crossed-transactions'. In these transactions an appropriate 'adult' question is asked but the response is emotional and impulsive as if the respondent is behaving as a child does in 'retorting' back to a parent. According to Berne, these crossed-transactions produce anxiety, stress and harm our social development. There may be any combination of transactions. A 'bossy' authoritarian question such as 'why don't you pull yourself together?' (parent to child) could be answered with 'I don't need you to tell me what to do!' (also parent to child). The central point in Berne's argument is that we have to analyse our communication and make our transactions 'adult to adult' (or appropriate) if we are to maximize our skills of interpersonal interaction. When we are working with children, it is important to ensure that our communication is appropriate so that the children are able to develop their social skills. It may not always be possible to have 'adult-to-adult' transactions within our professional interaction. There may be occasions when an especially insecure child is only capable of responding in a 'parent-to-child' manner. It can also be argued that there are a number of children who are never capable of having 'adult-to-adult', appropriate interaction because of the extent of their mental health needs. Nonetheless, it is important to recognize that we need to analyse our interaction and identify whenever it is possible to communicate with complementary transactions.

Berne has drawn attention to the psychological games that some people choose to play. He describes these encounters as 'ulterior transactions'. Ulterior transactions may appear to be 'adult to adult', but in reality they represent something else. The question 'My little angel, how do you feel today?!' may appear to be 'adult to adult' when in reality the person asking the question wants to be a nurturing parent to the child. This approach to working with children may not lead to the child developing adequate social skills, as the relationship always encourages dependence.

Reflective Activity 2.17

What can early years workers do to apply the ideas of Eric Berne to their professional practice?

Feedback

Part of the appeal of Berne's work is its simplicity. The theory is accessible and easy to understand. It is also important to ensure that the children you are working with behave in an appropriate way. Berne's work gives us a clear understanding of what is appropriate and what is not appropriate. Whatever happens, the interaction should always be appropriate. By being vigilant about what you are doing and what the children are doing and through asking whether you are being appropriate, a useful self-regulation of professional practice can occur. A difficulty in applying the work of Berne is that his theory may be seen as being impractical. It is difficult enough to identify the transactions (or examples of behaviour) in one child, let alone a class of up to thirty preschool children. This is the challenge in applying Berne's work when we are working with children and families. There is also the argument that little children are not aware of the subtle social nuances of the adult world. This is why they are little children! This limits our capacity to be completely assertive with the children we are working with.

Reflective Activity 2.18

How do the ideas of Berne help us to develop awareness of best practice and enhance our skills of employability.

Feedback

It can be argued that when we are working with children and families it is especially important to have good social skills. The social development of children is one of the four areas of the child we are hoping to nurture in our professional work. Moreover, in some professions, social skills are less important. A professional footballer is most concerned with the physical ability that enables an effective physical performance as an athlete. When we are working with children and families, it is very different. Our social skills need to be good so that we can help the children we are working with to develop accordingly.

The importance of effective communication for the developing child

Our communication skills are one of the defining characteristics of being human. This is why it is especially important to help children to develop effective communication skills. Upon becoming aware of key aspects of communication we are able to help children to grow and develop. This in turn increases our awareness of best practice when we are working with children and families alongside enhancing our employability prospects. Becoming aware of the forms of human communication is especially important when we are working with children and families.

Forms of verbal communication

Verbal communication refers to communication with words and conversation. Koprowska (2005, p.79) argues that 'providing information that is clear and context-related underpins … practice' when we are working with children and families. As with all forms of communication, there are some individuals who communicate effectively and others whose verbal communication skills need to be developed. Underdeveloped verbal skills may be a product of difficulties in relation to a number of important areas that are identified by Koprowska as including *listening, providing information; gathering information; paraphrasing and summarizing; using commands and corrective feedback; and bringing relationships to an end* (2005, p.72). It can be argued that when we are working with children and families, it is particularly important to have as highly developed skills as possible within these identified areas if our verbal communication is to be effective.

Koprowska (2005, p.77) identifies listening as being especially important in the process of communication. Listening is identified as being *an essential part of the turn-taking that characterizes human interaction*. When we are working with children and families, it is deemed as being particularly important to listen. Koprowska continues her argument by saying that listening enhances verbal interaction because when we listen to others we are effectively giving value to what others are saying. This enables us to 'hold' the child's *story in our mind and theirs* (2005, p.77). This in turn helps in identifying the processes that need to be made if we are to enhance our professional interaction.

In order to enhance verbal communication, it can be suggested that it is important to provide information that is readily understood. Koprowska (2005, p.79) emphasizes the significance of providing information that is factual. If our verbal communication is to be of a high standard, it is important that we provide facts at a pace that the child can manage. It is also important to provide verbal communication about boundaries. Koprowska (2005, p.79) argues that in the 'System for Analyzing Verbal Interaction', providing verbal boundaries is 'green light' behaviour because it is answering inner-person questions. *I am going to be with you for thirty minutes* is an example of verbal communication that provides a positive boundary. A further important way of enhancing verbal communication is to offer appropriate, effective explanations of professional practice. Many children and their families may not understand our professional work. It is, therefore, particularly important that children and families are made aware of the professional processes that are going to affect them when it is in their best interests to know about these processes. Koprowska (2005, p.80) goes on to emphasize the importance of 'opinions and proposals' in determining the effectiveness of communication. It is essential that we let children and families know about our opinions and proposals if the professional relationship is to be congruent. 'Proposals' ought to be thought of as being 'possibilities and choices' (2005, p.80) that are offered to children and families. In enhancing verbal communication it is also important to ensure that 'opinions' are supported by facts. Alongside these aspects of good practice, it is imperative that verbal communication communicates empathy. Koprowska (2005) emphasizes the importance of using empathic statements such as *I can see that this really has affected you*. Using verbal communication in this way can enhance the professional relationship and lead to best practice.

If we put good verbal skills into effect, our gathering of information is likely to be of a high standard. Koprowska (2005) draws attention to three different kinds of questions that are phrased as *narrow questions, broad questions and inner-person questions*. Narrow questions are very similar to closed questions as they can be answered using 'yes/no' answers. Broad questions are similar to open questions because they encourage others to give their views and opinions. Inner-person questions are phrased as being both narrow and broad. Their critical characteristic is that they aim to elicit individual feelings and emotions. Questions such as 'are you angry with me?' and 'how do you feel about living alone?' are examples of inner-person questions. It can be argued that they are especially good when we are working with children and families because they encourage the empathic process. The ideal is to try to develop this type of question at the expense of 'leading questions'. As Koprowska argues, leading questions such as 'don't you think it would be a good idea to go to the family centre?' do little other than coerce the other person into agreement (2005, p.84). They diminish the quality of verbal communication.

Koprowska (2005, p.87) draws attention to the importance of paraphrasing and summarizing if verbal communication is to be of a high standard. Paraphrasing can be understood as repeating to someone what they have said. It is an aspect of verbal communication that is considered to be important because it helps to check understanding and maximize interaction. Summarizing is equally important because it helps to communicate the individual's shared goals. In meetings with children and families, it is important to be aware of the disempowerment they may feel because they do not necessarily 'own the process'. By summarizing aims and objectives it becomes easier to lessen this feeling of disempowerment. If these skills of verbal communication can be combined with appropriate commands and corrective feedback, assertive verbal communication can be the central characteristic of working with children and families.

Koprowska (2005, p.89) draws attention to the importance of bringing working relationships to a positive end. It can be argued that if one's verbal skills are good, it is easier to provide an assertive conclusion to a working relationship. The ideal is to avoid unplanned endings, especially so that the relationship between the professional and the child does not break down. By considering what needs to be said at the conclusion of a meeting so that the encounter ends on a note of congruence, best practice can be put into effect.

Forms of non-verbal communication

Non-verbal communication is interpersonal communication that is not spoken including textual and other visual forms of communication. It is a form of communication that can also be defined as including communication by vocal sounds. Body language, eye contact, gaze, posture, body position, smell, touch, appearance, tone of voice and facial expressions are all important aspects of non-verbal communication influencing the service-user/social worker relationship. It is important to remember that non-verbal communication is often prompted by conversation. We hear someone's tone of voice and make a facial expression. We hear someone's verbal language and alter our body language accordingly. In other words, it can be argued that both non-verbal and non-vocal communication is often critically linked to verbal/vocal stimuli.

Koprowska (2005) has identified the importance of listening in enhancing the professional relationship between children and those who are working with them. It can be argued that listening depends upon aspects of non-verbal communication such as gesture and gaze, so it is essential that we are aware of how to support the listening process through effective non-verbal communication.

Some general guidance as to how to enhance non-verbal communication is possible, but it is also important to be aware that interpretations of non-verbal communication vary according to culture. As Knapp and Daly argue 'cultural characteristics serve as identity badges' (2011, p.258) in relation to interpersonal communication. In other words, what we interpret as appropriate non-verbal communication can be interpreted differently in another culture. Within the context of our work with children and families, it is important to be aware of body language, body position and posture. Too open or too closed body language is unlikely to facilitate a positive professional working relationship. Likewise, standing too close to a child or keeping too remote a distance can adversely affect the professional relationship. Either appearing to be too relaxed or too formal are both extreme messages that harm the communication between children and those who are working with them. It is also important to have appropriate eye contact. We should not 'stare' at our children but it is equally important to make appropriate eye contact. Both of these examples of non-verbal communication are likely to be interpreted negatively. It is important to strike some sort of balance so that the communication that is occurring appears to be as positive as possible.

It can be argued that appearance, smell, touch and facial expressions are other aspects of non-verbal communication that we should be aware of. Many children can have low self-esteem and if we reinforce this self-image by reacting negatively to a child's smell and/or appearance, the professional relationship is likely to be less than ideal. This does not mean that we avoid issues at the expense of being incongruent. It is more that we should use non-verbal communication in an assertive way so that touch and facial expressions contribute to the empathic relationship that rests at the centre of much positive professional practice.

Koprowska's work complements the earlier work of Michael Argyle (1988, Argyle and Colman 1995). Argyle emphasizes the importance of non-verbal communication (NVC) as it is deemed to be a particularly important aspect of human communication. This reinforces the argument that being aware of positive non-verbal communication is especially important when we are working with children and families. The expression of interpersonal attitudes and emotions has a particularly important influence on the professional/child relationship. The consequence is that in the context of this professional relationship our attitudes and feelings about our children (both positive and negative) are expressed by our NVC. How we look at a child and how we respond with our body language become especially important factors influencing the nature of the professional relationship. There is therefore a link between establishing a positive rapport with a child and the use of effective non-verbal communication.

A second important aspect of non-verbal communication is described by Argyle as being the function of 'self-presentation'. This refers to the image or impression that we want to communicate to others. For example, the way in which we dress can say much about what we value in the world. If we value traditional interpretations of discipline and punctuality, we may dress in a particular way in order to communicate this value. Likewise, if we do not value discipline and punctuality, we may choose to express this value judgement through the clothes we choose to wear. In a professional context this can have a significant impact upon the extent to which children and families are confident in our professional ability and/or is at ease with the professional relationship.

Argyle's and Colman (1995) work also reinforces Koprowska's point in relation to non-verbal behaviour supporting and/or complementing what is being communicated verbally. Argyle argues that when we are engaged in conversation with another person, our NVC can serve to control the synchronization of the interaction (for example, when it is time for one person to stop talking and another to begin), to provide feedback on what is being said by the speaker and to indicate whether or not the listener is attending to what is being said. If NVC is not used effectively it can affect interpersonal interaction adversely. NVC is therefore an extremely important aspect of the interaction occurring between professionals, children and families. According to Argyle, one of the most important roles of NVC is the expression of emotional states. NVC is a particularly important form of communication for professionals working with children and families because so much of our work relies upon responding effectively at an emotional level. Argyle also emphasizes the importance of NVC in managing relationships. Awareness of this aspect of communication will have inevitable consequences for the effectiveness or otherwise of the service-user/social worker relationship.

Summary of key points

In this chapter we have explored four important aspects of child development. We have looked at how children grow and develop physically, intellectually, emotionally and socially. We have identified some of the challenges that are present for us if we are working with children and families. There are still significant levels of poverty in families in the United Kingdom. The diets of children and families and the experience of domestic violence can become mitigating factors that prevent children from developing as they should. The chapter has also highlighted how the work of Piaget, Vygotsky, Gardner, Rogers and Berne can be applied to help us understand the intellectual, emotional and social development of children. If we combine these ideas with an awareness of the forms of communication that are used by children and families, we are more likely to meet the challenges of working effectively with children and families. This in turn results in best practice and enhances our employability.

Self-assessment questions

Question 1

What are the four main areas of child development we need to be aware of when we are working with children and families?

Question 2
What are the two main forms of communication identified in the chapter?

Question 3
Give an example concern for children's growth and development in each of the four areas discussed in this chapter (physical, intellectual, emotional and social development).

Moving on

This chapter has introduced you to how children grow and develop. Try to identify how some of the other theoretical content in this book can also be used to help explain children's growth and development.

Further reading

Lindon, J. (2012), *Understanding Child Development: 0–8 Years 3rd Edition: Linking Theory and Practice (LTP)*. London: Hodder Education.

An excellent textbook in terms of depth of content and analysis, and the material is always related to early years contexts.

Malim, T. and Birch, A. (1998), *Introductory Psychology*. London: Palgrave Macmillan.

An excellent textbook that is written in an accessible way and explains child development.

Ingleby, E. (2012), *Early Childhood Studies: A Social Science Perspective*. London: Bloomsbury.

Chapters on psychology sociology and social policy complement this chapter.

Best Practice and Enhancing Learning

3

Learning outcomes

After reading this chapter you should be able to:

- identify how key theories of learning (behaviourism, cognitive theory and humanism) have influenced our understanding of best practice in planning teaching and learning activities in early years;
- recognize how the application of Bloom's taxonomies of learning creates effective, differentiated learning outcomes;
- assess how key strategies can be applied in order to facilitate effective communication in the classroom.

Introduction

This chapter considers how and why shared understandings of best practice in teaching and learning have emerged. Geoff Petty (2009) explains the change in teaching and learning over time as being a change of perception of the teacher from being a 'sage on a stage' to a 'guide on the side'. Petty means that whereas the emphasis in the past was placed on 'learning through teachers', today's emphasis is placed much more on facilitating learning. The chapter outlines how and why this change in teaching philosophy has emerged by considering how behaviourist, cognitive and humanist theories of learning have shaped pedagogy. Anyone wanting to develop teaching skills within early years will be interested in the content of this chapter as it explores best practice within learning and teaching in early years. The chapter explores how key learning theories have evolved by considering how the theories can be applied within the classroom. A main theme of the chapter is the consideration of how pedagogy has been influenced by key learning theories. The consideration of theory and how it can be applied to practice will in turn help you with your curriculum planning and wider learning experiences. The application of Bloom's 'taxonomies of learning' model will help you to identify the importance of having clear, differentiated learning outcomes set at different levels in order to enable the facilitation of learning. The final section in this chapter explores key strategies for effective communication in the classroom. Effective communication skills are important if we are to facilitate learning in early years. This aspect of pedagogy is important for education in general and requires us to reflect on the development of the children's general communication skills.

Theories of learning: Behaviourism

According to behaviourist psychologists such as Skinner, learning is defined as being a relatively permanent change in behaviour brought about as a result of experience or practice. Behaviourists recognize that learning is an internal event. Learning, however, depends upon the display of overt behaviour.

Learning by association

The term 'learning theory' is often associated with behaviourism. Learning theory investigates how the environment influences behaviour.

This makes behaviourism different to other explanations for learning such as 'biological maturation' or 'genetics' due to the emphasis that is placed on the importance of the environment.

If we are asked to think of a marketing logo, we can probably identify a brand name and see the image 'in our head'. We are so used to seeing these images in the media and around our daily environment that we do not need the company name to recognize what is being advertised. This is because we have learnt the company name through association. We now associate the logo/picture with the organization. Advertising can play a significant role in conditioning us. The media and marketing groups pair a stimulus (the product) with a conditioned response. A new car (a neutral stimulus) is associated with a positive conditioned stimulus (models, fun, and holidays for example). Summer holidays are advertised with 'good weather', 'lovely beaches', 'nice hotels' and the image of 'having a good time'. The reverse can also happen: in other words, creating negative associations such as in political advertising (pairing something unpleasant with a particular party).

Examples of learning by association and education

An example of learning by association and education can occur if children learn a particular subject because they unconsciously associate it with a teacher they like. Another example of learning by association is when teachers follow particular routines in order to show the children what they are expected to do. A teacher may stand in a particular area of the classroom in order to get the children's attention. A particular form of music may be played in order to get the children to go quiet. Learning through the use of mnemonics is another example of learning through association. This may take the form of associating a difficult spelling with a phrase or sentence, so for example the word *science* could be broken down into:

Science Can Interest Every Nosy Child Everywhere

Classical conditioning

Classical conditioning is a type of learning that is associated with the behaviourist school of thought. As behaviourism is one of the earliest pedagogical learning theories, it is referred to as a classical theory. One of the main theorists who is associated with the development of classical conditioning is Ivan

Pavlov, a Russian scientist trained in biology and medicine. Pavlov studied the digestive system of dogs. He became intrigued with the factors influencing dogs' salivation. Upon investigating this phenomenon, Pavlov established the laws of classical conditioning.

During Pavlov's investigations he discovered that an 'unconditioned stimulus' (for example, food) will naturally (without learning) elicit or bring about an 'unconditioned response' (for example, salivation). Pavlov's studies with dogs revealed that a natural response occurs to an unconditioned stimulus. However, over time this unconditioned stimulus can combine with other factors in order to elicit what is referred to as a 'conditioned response'. If, for example, a dog is given food every time a bell is rung, the dog will eventually salivate when the bell is rung. The food is the unconditioned stimulus and the salivation is the reflexive response. When the dog salivates upon hearing a bell, this represents an example of a 'conditioned response' to a 'conditioned stimulus'. The bell is the conditioned stimulus and the salivation is the conditioned response.

If we apply this theory to early years pedagogy, classical conditioning is seen primarily in the conditioning of emotional behaviour. Factors influencing our emotions become associated with neutral stimuli that gain our attention. For example, the school, classroom, teacher or subject matter are initially neutral stimuli that gain attention. Activities at school or in the classroom automatically elicit emotional responses and these activities are associated with the neutral or orienting stimulus. After repeated exposure to the stimuli, the previously neutral response will elicit the emotional response.

Example:

- A child is bullied at school.
- The child feels bad when bullied.
- The child associates being bullied with school.
- The child begins to feel bad when they think of school.

In order to extinguish the association of 'feeling bad' and 'thinking of school', the connection between school and being bullied must be broken.

Operant conditioning

Operant conditioning can be defined as a type of learning in which behaviour is strengthened if it is followed by a 'reinforcer' (reward) or diminished if followed by a 'punishment'. Operant conditioning tends to be associated with situations in which a choice of behaviour is possible. This form of conditioning has become especially important in early years pedagogy. We can associate operant conditioning with best practice. Operant conditioning techniques attempt to regulate the choices being made by the individual. A central part of operant conditioning is to consider the ways in which the environment produces consequences. It is important to distinguish between the 'who' and the 'what' that is being 'reinforced', 'punished' or 'extinguished'. Additionally, reinforcement, punishment and extinction are not terms restricted to experiments. Naturally occurring consequences can also be said to 'reinforce', 'punish' or 'extinguish' behaviour and these consequences are not always delivered by people. 'Reinforcement' causes behaviour to occur with greater frequency whereas 'punishment' results in behaviour occurring with less frequency. 'Extinction' refers to the lack of any consequence following a type of behaviour. When behaviour is inconsequential, producing neither favourable nor unfavourable consequences, it will occur with less frequency. A central theme within operant conditioning is that if a previously reinforced behaviour is no longer reinforced with either positive or negative reinforcement, it results in a decline in the response. One of the psychologists associated with operant conditioning is Burrhus Skinner. Skinner believed that internal thoughts and motivations could not be used to explain behaviour. Instead, he suggested, we should look at the external, observable causes of human behaviour.

Skinner's box

When we apply operant conditioning, we look to reinforce behaviour that complies with our expectations. We also seek to punish behaviour that does not comply with our expectations. The thinking behind operant conditioning is that reinforced behaviours will occur more frequently, while punished and extinguished behaviours will be performed less often. An example of operant conditioning is a rat learning to navigate through a maze more quickly and efficiently after a number of attempts. A 'Skinner box', used to study these concepts, is a box that houses an animal such as a rat and offers both unconditioned and conditioned stimuli – such as coloured lights and food, respectively – and response levers or keys that serve to monitor the animal's behaviour. A Skinner box may be used to test classical conditioning in a bird by associating a red light with each 'feed', eventually causing the bird to peck not only at food, but upon seeing the red light. A Skinner box may be fairly simple, with only one lever or key or it may be quite complex, with a variety of stimuli and ways of monitoring responses. The Skinner box has received criticism because it does not capture every aspect of the animal's behaviour.

Pushing the lever with a nose or a paw registers as the same response, for example, and light touches of the lever may not be recorded.

Applications of operant conditioning

Superstitious behaviour

Superstitions that are reinforced can have a similar effect. For example, some students might go to an exam with a 'lucky pen' because they used the pen previously and it is associated with getting a positive result.

Behaviour management

We can use a 'punishment' to manage classroom behaviour: for example, if a child is constantly late for class, you may want to use a negative reinforcement such as 'no break' or 'missing ten minutes of their lunch time break'. If this strategy is adhered to for all the children who are late, the inappropriate behaviour is likely to decrease.

Pedagogical best practice based on behaviourism

- Teaching by shaping desired behaviour – rewards and punishments.
- Awareness of how the classroom environment influences learning and teaching (for example Montessori based approaches to teaching that have an 'uncluttered' classroom environment in order to stimulate individual learning from the child).
- Being a role model by personifying appropriate behaviour.
- Tests – often involving memory (remember the mnemonics).
- Step-by-step approaches to learning.
- Breaking big tasks into bite size tasks in order to allow for frequent experiences of success.
- Quick feedback in order to motivate the children.
- Demonstrating how to complete tasks.
- Allowing learners to practice.

Operant conditioning: A pedagogical overview

If behaviour is reinforced, it is more likely to be repeated. If you are applying operant conditioning to teaching in early years, it is important for reinforcement to follow the desired behaviour as soon as possible. It is also important to ensure that consistency characterizes the behaviour programme if it is to be a success.

Positive reinforcement

We can provide positive reinforcement when we are teaching in early years in a variety of ways. These ways can include verbal praise, giving good grades for good work and using non-verbal cues (nodding, smiling, raising eyebrows).

Negative reinforcement

We can also reinforce behaviour in 'negative' ways by offering a 'threat' or 'punishment'.

Punishment

Punishing children is not associated with 'best practice'. This is because the general pedagogical ideal is that children should be learning 'what to do' as opposed to 'what not to do'.

Teaching activities applying operant conditioning

There are a number of example teaching activities that apply operant conditioning. Some of these activities include the following:

- 'Skills and drills' (repetitive exercises) using worksheets. In early years pedagogy, this may take place with mathematical teaching.
- 'Programmed instruction' through memorizing information.
- 'Role play' (realistic practice) through modelling.
- Multiple choice questions that practice key skills.
- Step-by-step approaches exemplified by teacher talk.
- 'Token economies' where positive behaviour is rewarded by receiving a desirable token such as a desirable 'badge' and punished through denying the child the token.

Applying operant conditioning in the classroom

Children can be influenced by their classroom experiences in a profound way. The following recommendations for best practice pedagogy are based on the application of principles of operant conditioning.

- It is important to stress key points by summarizing at both the beginning and the end of a teaching session.
- It is also important to praise and encourage (past success provides motivation for present learning!).

- Make sure that you set clear objectives and use these to measure students' achievement.
- Allow time for practice, not just theory.

Criticisms of behaviourist approaches to teaching

There are a number of criticisms of behaviourist educational approaches. These include:

- Behaviourist education tends to be teacher led and centred on the teacher.
- This may generate a passive view of the children as learners because they are regarded as being 'shaped by the learning environment'.
- The application of operant conditioning techniques such as token economy can be regarded as being authoritarian because the teacher is essentially manipulating the learning process. This can represent a disempowerment of the learner.
- External reinforcement is used to motivate learners as opposed to encouraging internal motivation. This approach to learning can in turn remove freedom from the learning process.

Cognitive learning theory

Cognitive theory is based on the assumption that there are thought processes behind human behaviour. An important component of cognitive theory is the Gestalt theories of perception that explore how the brain imposes patterns on the perceived world. These Gestalt theories of perception are often associated with problem-solving learning. Cognitive theory is also influenced by the developmental psychology of Piaget through focusing on the maturational factors that influence human understanding. Broadly speaking, cognitive theory is interested in how people understand the world around them and in their aptitude and capacity to learn. Cognitive theory is also interested in learning styles and it is the fundamental basis of the educational approach known as constructivism. This aspect of education emphasizes the role of the learner in constructing his or her own ideas and the factors influencing this process.

Memory

The 'memory' is a very complex human function that is much researched and is of tremendous interest to cognitive theorists. Memory is also of central importance to learning. Indeed, learning depends upon the memory with the process of 'memorizing' being part of one of the lowest levels of rote learning. Memorizing begins with a sensory buffer. Part of the information being memorized stays in the brain for about 1/15th of a second, while the brain assembles it to 'make sense'. Most of us will have experienced the illusion by which a succession of still pictures presented rapidly enough appears to be moving as it is the basis of all cinematography. Once the frame rate drops below about sixteen frames per second, however, we may well become conscious of the flicker or jumps from one still image to another. Similarly, we do not hear a succession of speech sounds but complete words or phrases. It is as if the brain waits to assemble a meaningful sound before passing it on to the next stage which is short-term memory (STM). The human STM appears to deal best with sounds rather than visual stimuli, but this may be due to the fact that visual stimuli are taken in all at once, whereas sounds are processed in a linear fashion – over time. In actual fact the STM is able to hold material for about fifteen to thirty seconds, although this can be expanded by practice. This is much shorter than we may initially realize. In general, the human memory has a capacity to memorize in the region of seven items (plus or minus two). 'Items' are defined by meaning rather than size, so it may be difficult to remember telephone numbers of more than seven digits, but if '01234' is remembered as the 'dialling code', it becomes just one item and remembering the subsequent numbers '7,9,3,1,5,6' becomes simpler. If this sequence of numbers is in turn 'chunked' (or 'associated') as being 'my work phone number', it becomes even easier to remember. This of course assumes that a label for the 'chunk' already exists in long-term memory (LTM). Theoretically, LTM has infinite capacity and lasts for the rest of your life. Tulving (1985) has suggested the useful distinction between three components of LTM:

- *Semantic* memory that stores concepts and ideas.
- *Episodic* (sometimes referred to as 'autobiographical' or 'narrative') memory that contains memories of events.
- *Procedural* memory concerns skills and 'know-how' rather than 'know-that' knowledge.

People with amnesia, for example, typically lose episodic memory, but other aspects of their memory may be relatively intact. Episodic and semantic memory are more prone to distortion than procedural memory, which is more robust. According to Atherton (2009), a skill lost through lack of practice typically comes back rapidly when called upon and without significant degradation. However, semantic and episodic memories are more amenable to linguistic description and communication.

Memory involves storing and retrieving data. We can't remember everything which can be frustrating in certain situations (for example, where did we put that lesson plan that worked so well last year?!). This is because it is impossible to deal with all the information we receive. This can mean that efficient memory relies on forgetting lots of unimportant information but remembering key facts. As memory is linked to learning, this means that it is affected by a number of factors. These include:

- Practice – the more times a piece of information is encountered, the more likely it will be committed to LTM.
- Stage theory – information passes through STM on its way to LTM.
- Primacy – the first thing in a list is remembered well.
- Recency/retention – the last thing encountered is remembered well.

Reflective Activity 3.1

Is it possible to read the following?

How can you raed tihs pciee of inofmtoin wehn the wrdos are all jmumbeld up?
Is teher a paettren?
Can you sopt it?

Feedback

When the first and last letters of a word stay the same but the letters in the middle of the word are jumbled up, the brain can still perceive the word that it has learnt by building up from previous knowledge and LTM.

This shows that memory involves encoding, storage and retrieval, but you can't have retrieval unless you go through the process of encoding and storing.

Cognitive pedagogy: Best practice and early years

Cognitive strategies are still teacher led, but learning is far more active for the learners. The learners are more involved in lessons, and they are given tasks, for example problem solving. Gestalt principles are based on recommending that learners should be encouraged to discover the underlying nature of a topic or problem (in other words, the relationship between the component parts). Instruction should be based on the laws of organization so that there is clear planning with learners in order to organize new learning by connecting it to previous learning.

The cognitive approach is more of an academic approach based on the principle that learning occurs primarily through exposure to logically presented information. A good analogy that helps in understanding the cognitive approach is to visualize two buckets. Imagine the full bucket of the effective teacher pouring its contents into the empty bucket of the less informed learner. Cognitivism can be understood as being the 'tell' approach to learning, so its predominant learning activity is the lecture or didactic teaching approach. Current teaching trends, however, are not always in favour of this approach to teaching and recommend shorter, 'mini-lectures' geared to an internet multimedia culture. The application of teacher led pedagogy within early years is important, but the amount of didactic teaching being delivered to children needs to take into consideration the concentration levels of the children. Children aged 0–8 can only be 'lectured' to for so long!

Cognitive techniques used in the classroom

These include:

- Montessori approaches to teaching with its emphasis on 'practical learning'. Children are asked to solve problems with 'props' in order to stimulate cognitive development;
- diagrams;
- films;
- talks by subject specialists;
- class presentations;
- oral storytelling.

Some of the advantages of using a cognitive curriculum or approach include that the curriculum is built on a base of knowledge to extend learners' knowledge or information on concepts and rules. It can provide the rationale upon which the learner can build active learning strategies. This may mean that it is seen as a more rapid learning method than behaviourist or humanist methods of learning.

Applying cognitive learning to pedagogy to ensure best practice in early years

The following guidelines apply if you are applying cognitive learning to early years.

- Becoming aware of the Montessori methods of facilitating problem solving through the use of 'props'. Learning and teaching becomes as practical as possible.
- Information should be presented logically.
- Build from an initial base of information.
- Relationships between 'bits of information' are important.
- The curriculum needs to be organized to reveal its construction.
- As meaning is constructed, we need to learn a variable amount of different information.
- We need to develop children as 'thinkers' if they are to become learners.
- We need to develop strategies and skills in pedagogy to enable children to learn effectively.
- Videos, class demonstrations, oral readings and discussions help the learning process.

Like behaviourism, cognitive learning approaches are predominantly teacher led, but the learning process tends to be more active for the children. The children are expected to be more involved in lessons and they are given tasks such as problem solving activities. These activities are based on the idea that there are thought processes behind behaviour and that changes in behaviour are observed as an indicator of what is going on in the children's minds. Cognitive learning encourages children to discover the underlying nature of a topic or problem (in other words, the relationship) and cognitive pedagogy attempts to build learning around a base of logical organization. For Petty (2009), cognitivist theorists base their ideas about pedagogy on a belief that education is more than simply communicating facts and procedures to memory. Its main objective is to develop children's independent thinking skills. This is similar to the idea that children can only be 'educated' when they have forgotten what has been learned.

Humanist pedagogical theory

According to Carl Rogers (1983), the importance of 'teaching' is often overestimated. The key principle according to Rogers is what he refers to as the 'facilitation' of learning. This third approach to best practice and learning considered in the chapter is very different to the behaviourist emphasis that is placed on the environmental factors influencing teaching and learning. Both behaviourist and cognitive approaches to learning adopt something of a scientific approach in terms of the methods they use and the theories that they generate. In contrast, the humanist approach can be described as being 'anti-scientific' in the way in which it investigates human beings. The underpinning belief is that we are all unique individuals. Humanism is based on the belief that we are the product of our own particular circumstances. Atkinson et al. (1993) identify that humanism attempts to understand the individual by identifying 'subjective experiences' in order to consider individual thoughts and emotions. Humanist learning theory was developed in America from 1960 onwards and the theory is associated with two psychologists, Carl Rogers and Abraham Maslow. Rogers is associated with 'client-centred learning' and Maslow considers the 'hierarchy' of learning needs. Humanists regard humans as needing to become proactive individuals who are then able to apply 'free will' to their behaviour. Petty (2009) summarizes this approach to understanding humans by emphasizing the importance of making appropriate choices within the learning process. Moreover, the term 'humanist' is generally associated with a variety of approaches that are applied to studying aspects of human behaviour. This provides a holistic approach to studying human behaviour through an emphasis that is placed on the importance of studying the entire person. Humanist theories of learning tend to be value-driven. Although there is an acceptance of a 'natural' desire to learn, there is also an emphasis placed upon empowering learners with a facilitating teacher being of central importance to the learning process.

Carl Rogers and Malcolm Knowles

Carl Rogers is associated with the development of humanistic approaches to education. These theories of education are at the centre of much best practice within teaching and learning. Humanist theories of learning place an emphasis on 'what should happen' as opposed to 'what does happen'. The key phrase associated with humanist learning is 'facilitating learning', with teachers being encouraged to empower a situation of self-directed learning. This process results in the teacher needing to take a 'step back' and instead of leading the learning, there is an emphasis placed on facilitating learning processes.

Rogers distinguishes two types of learning. There is 'cognitive learning' (academic knowledge such as psychology or multiplication tables) and 'experiential learning' (applied knowledge such as learning about engines in order to repair a car). The key to the distinction is that experiential learning addresses the needs and wants of the learner and is equivalent to personal change and growth. Rogers believes that all human beings have a natural desire to learn, so this means that the role of the teacher is to facilitate learning. In helping to facilitate learning, it is important to become aware of the following key aspects of the learning process.

- Set a positive climate for learning.
- Clarify the purposes of the learning.
- Organize and make available appropriate learning resources.
- Balance the intellectual and emotional components of learning.
- Share feelings and thoughts with learners without dominating them.

For Rogers, learning is likely to be facilitated when:

- the student participates completely in the learning process and has control over its nature and direction;
- the learning process is concerned with practical, social, personal or research interests;
- self-evaluation becomes a principal method of assessing progress or success.

Rogers also emphasizes the importance of 'learning to learn' through being open to change. Rogerian learning is therefore based on psychotherapy and humanistic approaches to psychology. It is a profound theory of learning that has influenced pedagogy. Further key ideas include that:

- significant learning takes place when the subject matter is relevant to the personal interests of the student;
- learning which is threatening to the self (for example new attitudes or perspectives) are more easily assimilated when external threats are at a minimum;
- learning proceeds faster when the threat to the self is low;
- self-initiated learning is the most lasting and pervasive form of learning.

Humanist learning theory applies the ideas of other leading humanist theorists such as Malcolm Knowles and Abraham Maslow. Knowles attempts to develop a distinctive conceptual basis for pedagogy through consideration of 'self-direction' and on 'group work'. The ideas of Knowles have led to a reconsideration of the concept of 'education' through emphasizing the importance of 'helping learners to learn'. Knowles' learning theory has seven main assumptions linked to motivation.

1. *Learners should acquire as much self-understanding as possible.* The importance of understanding needs, motivations, interests, capacities and goals is emphasized. Learners are encouraged to be viewed in an objective and appropriate way. According to Knowles, the learning process should be based on 'acceptance' and 'respect'.

2. *Learners should develop an attitude of acceptance and respect towards others.* This is viewed by Knowles as being the attitude on which all human relations depend. Learning is based on distinguishing between human beings and

learning concepts. It is regarded as being important to challenge ideas without displaying confrontation. Ideally, this attitude will develop from acceptance, love, and respect, into empathy and the sincere desire to help others.

3. *Learners should develop a dynamic attitude toward life.* There ought to be acceptance of change and the developing awareness that the learning process depends on change. Every experience is visualized as being an opportunity to learn as learning skills develop from this experience.

4. *The learning process depends upon considering the causes, not the symptoms, of behaviour.* Solutions to problems lie in their causes, not in their symptoms. Knowles considers that this aspect of education is a critical component of the learning process.

5. *Learning depends on acquiring the skills necessary to realize individual potential.* Knowles considers that every person has the capability to make a positive contribution to society. Realizing one's potential requires skills of many kinds. These skills include vocational, social, recreational and artistic attributes. A main purpose of teaching and learning is considered to be enabling individuals to acquire the skills necessary to develop individual potential.

6. *Learners need to ultimately understand the essential values that are central in helping to promote a positive learning experience.* They should be familiar with the heritage of knowledge, the great ideas and the great traditions of the world in which they live. If this idea is applied to early years it is more associated with laying appropriate foundations for learning. This entails becoming aware of the moral values that bind humans together.

7. *Learners should understand that their social circumstances direct social changes.* In a democratic society (that is Knowles's ideal society), people of all ages participate in making decisions that influence the whole of society. This makes it imperative for basic political, economic and social knowledge to be developed as part of the learning process.

Applying humanist learning to enable best practice for pedagogy in early years

These humanist principles can be considered for any learning activity. At the beginning of any lesson a teacher needs to:

- Become aware of approaches of teaching and learning that are based on individual affective development. The Regio Emilia approach developed by Loris Malaguzzi is based on treating children as individuals. A self-guided curriculum is encouraged that is based on principles of respect and responsibility. The educational philosophy of Rudolf Steiner is also based on enabling children to develop as individuals. In this approach to teaching and learning, children are encouraged to develop as unique individuals.

- Establish a climate of equality and mutual respect.
- Determine the expectations of the children.
- Involve the children in planning the objectives of the lesson.
- Acknowledge the value of their learning experiences.

This application of humanistic pedagogy can help in developing key teaching and learning themes.

Abraham Maslow

Abraham Maslow's hierarchy of needs is represented in the shape of a pyramid, with the largest and lowest levels of needs at the bottom and the need for self-actualization at the top. When Maslow's ideas are applied to pedagogy, each component of the hierarchy of needs can be associated with an aspect of pedagogy.

At the base of the pyramid of needs, Maslow refers to the importance of meeting 'physiological' or biological needs if learning is to develop. These physiological needs can be met in early years education in the following ways:

- reduced price and free lunch programmes;
- correct room temperatures;
- sufficient toilet breaks;
- refreshment breaks.

Maslow also makes reference to the importance of ensuring that safety is an essential part of the pedagogical process. In early years pedagogy, this idea can be applied in the following ways:

- lessons need to be well planned and delivered in a coherent way;
- classroom behaviour needs to be managed and regulated accordingly;
- emergency procedures need to be planned, discussed and rehearsed;
- discipline needs to be applied fairly;
- expectations need to be reasonable;
- teacher attitudes ought to be based on being as 'accepting' and non-judgemental as possible;
- pedagogy ought to be based on giving praise for appropriate responses as opposed to punishing inappropriate responses.

Maslow also emphasizes the importance of engendering feelings of love and belonging within the learning process. With regards to teacher–student relationships, it becomes important for the teacher to develop a number of key aspects of pedagogy. These include the development of:

- empathetic relationships that are considerate and express interest in individuals;
- skilled methods of one-on-one instruction;
- positive comments and constructive feedback;
- knowledge of children's likes, dislikes and concerns;
- pastoral and personal skills alongside academic skills;
- listening skills in order to meet student needs;
- supportive relationships with students;
- appropriate assistance for learning support;
- awareness of students' thoughts, opinions and judgements;
- trust in children by providing opportunities for responsibility.

With regard to the relationships between children within the class, it becomes important to ensure that a number of key pedagogical principles are followed that are based on what Maslow would describe as 'establishing emotional security'. These principles ought to be applied during:

- class meetings;
- class discussions;
- situations requiring mutual trust;
- 'show-and-tell' and sharing activities.

Esteem

Humanist learning emphasizes the importance of developing 'self-esteem' within the learning process. A number of key aspects of pedagogy can help in developing learners' self-esteem so that the children become more confident about the learning process in general. It is important to ensure that the development of new knowledge is based on what has been previously learned in order to help ensure the development of the 'scaffolding' process of learning. It is also vital to:

- focus on the learning strengths of the children and their key learning abilities;
- take individual needs and abilities into account when planning lessons and carrying them out;
- teach and model helpful learning strategies for the children (for example making sure that you are able to demonstrate what the children are expected to do when they are learning);

- base new teaching, strategies and plans on manageable learning outcomes;
- be alert to children's difficulties with the learning process so that you can intervene and help as soon as possible;
- be available and approachable so that those children having difficulties with learning feel comfortable and able to 'ask for help';
- involve all the children in classroom activities;
- apply discipline as appropriately as possible;
- gain respect from others in order to develop a classroom environment where the children are 'positive' as opposed to being 'judgemental';
- provide rewards for completing work well;
- establish a fair system for rewards and punishments;
- develop and apply a curriculum that enables children to become empathetic and effective listeners;
- apply cooperative learning in such a way as to develop trust between children;
- involve children in activities that they see as being 'important' and 'worthwhile'.

Knowledge and understanding

There are a number of key principles that form the basis of developing knowledge and understanding within humanist approaches to learning. The following key principles are of particular importance:

- allow students time to explore areas of curiosity;
- deliver teaching sessions that provide an intellectual challenge;
- plan and prepare lessons that connect areas of learning so that the children are able to compare and contrast ideas;
- use an interactive approach to pedagogy whenever possible;
- enable the children to approach topics of learning from as many various angles as possible;
- provide opportunities for philosophical thought and discussion where appropriate;
- involve the children in learning activities that challenge their existing knowledge and understanding in an appropriate way.

Aesthetic learning

Humanist pedagogy places an importance on developing the appreciation of human aesthetic qualities. This leads to an emphasis being placed on the following pedagogical aspects of the learning process.

- Classroom materials ought to be arranged in a manner that is neat and 'easy on the eye'.

- Children's work ought to be displayed regularly if it shows the development and emergence of aesthetic qualities.
- 'Colourful' and 'bright' displays reveal that children are being enabled to apply their aesthetic abilities.
- Learning materials ought to be updated in order to ensure that they do not become 'out of date'.
- Teaching rooms need to be designed so that they create 'varied', 'appealing' and 'interesting' learning areas (for example the main teaching room may be painted in colours that 'soften' the atmosphere, such as 'light blue').
- Large window areas let in light in order to stimulate learning.
- Well-maintained physical surroundings (clean rooms, keeping walls painted, desks clean and repaired) can help in promoting a positive learning environment.

Self-actualization

The ultimate goal of humanist learning is for the pedagogical process to enable the children to learn as independently as possible. This is at the heart of the meaning of the important humanist idea of 'self-actualization'. Once learners become 'self-actualized', they are associated with the following attributes:

- the pedagogical process provides children with the freedom to explore learning and discover on their own;
- learning becomes meaningful and connects 'real-life experiences';
- teaching sessions enable the children to become involved in projects that help them to develop their powers of self-expression.

Humanists consider humans to be proactive unique individuals who exercise free will over their behaviour. Petty (2009) emphasizes the importance that 'choice' plays in enabling this ability to learn. The argument is developed that choice enables learners to engage with the learning process in an intense, personal way. Humanism emphasizes the importance of drawing on experiences and interaction in order to develop critical thinking, initiative and self-directed learning.

Learning theories review

The various learning theories have advantages and disadvantages. Becoming aware of these advantages and disadvantages is essential in order to be aware of best practice with teaching and learning.

Behaviourist learning

Key Idea: Learning occurs primarily through the reinforcement of desired responses.

Pedagogical Assumption: Learning can produce a relatively permanent change in behaviour.

Key Terms: Behaviour; Conditioning; Reinforcement; Learning Hierarchies.

Cognitive learning

Key Idea: Learning occurs primarily through exposure to logically presented information.

Pedagogical Assumption: Learning is based on the process of constructing new meaning.

Key Terms: Cognition, Discovery Learning, Insightful Learning, Meaningful Learning.

Humanist learning

Key Idea: Learning occurs primarily through reflection on personal experience.

Pedagogical Assumption: Learning is a process of self-development.

Key Terms: Self-Actualization, Individual Needs, Intrinsic Motivation.

Surface and deep learning

A general idea in pedagogical theory is that a learner's conception of what learning is can impact the quality of their learning. This idea is revealed in what is referred to as 'the Jabberwocky exercise'.

Reflective Activity 3.2

Read the passage below and answer the following questions:

Twas brillig, and the slithy toves
Did gyre and gimble in the wabe
All mimsy were the borogoves
And the mome raths outgrabe

Question 1: What were the slithy toves doing in the wabe?
Question 2: How would you describe the state of the borogoves?

⇨

Question 3: What can you say about the mome raths?

Question 4: Why were the borogroves mimsy?

Question 5: How effective was the mome raths' strategy?

Most people get the following answers:

Answer to Question 1: Gyring and gambling.

Answer to Question 2: They are all mimsy.

Answer to Question 3. They outgrabe.

Reflection

Questions 4 and 5 are impossible to answer as it is impossible to fully comprehend the text. The only meaning we are able to find is based on pure speculation. The purpose of the activity is designed to show you that for lower learning (or what is referred to as 'surface learning') we do not require learners to make 'sense of material'. Those tasks which require deeper learning require students to make meanings or 'constructs'. Learning without understanding is called rote learning, or surface learning. This is where the learner does not need to make sense of the material in order to get the right answer.

The general idea in pedagogy is that there are five levels of surface and deep learning. Levels 1–3 are 'surface' learning whereas levels 4–5 represent deep learning.

Level 1: Learning leads to an increase in knowledge.

Level 2: Learning leads to 'memorizing' information.

Level 3: Learning is based on acquiring facts or procedures which are to be applied.

Level 4: Learning is based on making sense of concepts. Learners make active attempts to construct 'meaning'.

Level 5: Learning is based on trying to understand 'reality'. Marton and Saljo (1984) summarize this idea when they argue that when you have really learnt something, you see things that you couldn't see before. This leads to a completely different view of the world.

Surface learning can be described as 'shallow' or 'superficial' learning as it is based on recalling factual information. In many forms of formal pedagogy in early years, children need to be able to memorize and regurgitate information in order to complete 'memory tests'. As this type of learning involves 'learning by memory', it makes no links to themes or concepts and the learning process is passive. In contrast, deeper learning requires the organization and structuring of information in order to utilize existing knowledge and understanding. This allows learners to form new concepts by challenging existing knowledge.

Taxonomies of learning

Benjamin Bloom is famous for his identification of what are referred to as key domains of educational activities. These educational activities are:

- *Cognitive*: mental skills (*Knowledge*).
- *Affective*: growth in feelings or emotional areas (*Attitude*).
- *Psychomotor*: manual or physical skills (*Skills*).

Bloom emphasizes the importance that education has in realizing 'mastery' of subjects and the promotion of higher forms of thinking rather than a simple transferring of facts. Bloom demonstrated that most teaching tends to be focused on 'fact transfer' and 'information recall'. This is referred to as the lowest level of training as opposed to 'true meaningful personal development' and to this day, this remains a central challenge for teachers and educators.

Bloom's notion of 'taxonomies of learning' links directly back to the concept of 'domains of learning'. The concept can be developed to consider how we can encourage deeper learning in pedagogy through applying the learning taxonomies.

The major categories in the psychomotor domain (listed in increasing order of difficulty – surface to deep learning) are as follows:

1. Imitation – observes skill and tries to repeat it.
2. Manipulation – performs skill according to instruction rather than observation.
3. Precision – reproduces a skill with accuracy, proportion and exactness.
4. Articulation – combines one or more skills in sequence with harmony and consistency.
5. Naturalization – Completes one or more skills with ease and becomes 'automatic'.

The major categories in the cognitive domain (listed in increasing order of difficulty – surface to deep learning) include:

1. Knowledge – recognition and recall of information.
2. Comprehension – interpret, translate or summarize information.

3. Application – use information in a situation different from the original learning context.
4. Analysis – separates the whole into parts until relationships are clear.
5. Synthesis – combines elements to form a new entity from an original one.
6. Evaluation – involves acts of decision making or judging based on criteria or a rationale.

The major categories in the affective domain: (listed in increasing order of difficulty – surface to deep learning) include:

1. Receiving – being passively aware of certain stimuli, through learning activities such as listening.
2. Responding – complying with expectations by creating stimuli that are anticipated.
3. Valuing – displaying behaviour consistent with shared beliefs or attitudes.
4. Organizing – commitment to 'set values' that are reinforced by behaviour.
5. Characterizing – behaviour is completely consistent with internalized values.

At its basic level, Bloom's Taxonomy provides a simple, quick and easy checklist to help you develop your pedagogical learning outcomes in order to produce best practice. You can use the increasing difficulty scale to differentiate between your learners, offering challenge to some and less challenge to other more needy learners. The more detailed elements within each domain provide additional reference points for learning design and evaluation, whether for a single lesson, session or activity or for an entire early years syllabus. At its most complex, Bloom's Taxonomy can be described as a continuously evolving form of pedagogical theory. At its most practical application, the concepts can lead to the most wonderful and inspiring pedagogy with children in early years.

If we apply Bloom's ideas, we can ensure that we move our pedagogical learning from a 'surface' approach to a 'deeper' understanding and application. A 'deep' approach to pedagogy produces longer lasting learning, and in general deep learners engage with pedagogy more than surface learners. Deep learners structure their understanding of concepts whereas surface learners tend to just remember unstructured detail. It is generally accepted that deep learners make connections with previous learning whereas surface learners do not have this pedagogical characteristic. Surface learning produces marginally higher scores on tests of factual recall immediately after studying. However, surface learners forget this quickly and as little as a week later, deep learners score higher even in tests of factual recall. Bloom's Taxonomy reveals that most learners can adopt both a surface and a deep approach to their learning. Children have been found to make their learning choice in association with the nature of the assessment and the teacher's expectation of learning requirements. This reveals the potential that pedagogy has to develop learners' deep learning skills when these learners arrive with basic surface learning skills.

Methods that encourage deep learning

There are a number of pedagogical strategies that help to develop 'deep learning'.

1. Create intrinsic motivation. Intrinsic motivation refers to an interest in the subject and the tasks in themselves. Try to develop curiosity, interest, passion and 'real world implications' in your teaching and learning activities. Try to develop teaching and learning activities that are based on creativity, problem solving and individual responses to the pedagogical materials.
2. Plan learner activity. Children need to be 'active' rather than 'passive learners' if they are to enjoy learning. Activities ought to be planned, reflected upon and processed.
3. Encourage/promote/initiate interaction with others. Group work requires negotiating meaning, expressing and manipulating ideas. Discussion can be used in order to promote high quality learning.
4. Establish a good knowledge base. Without existing concepts, it is impossible to make sense of new concepts. It is vital that the children's existing knowledge and experience are brought out in the learning process. The structure of the topic must be made clear so that the learning process can be understood.

Practical strategies encouraging deep learning

Make sure that your pedagogy is based on 'teaching by asking' as opposed to 'teaching by telling'. Try to adopt the 'pose, pause and pounce' technique when you are asking questions to children. In other words, ask a question and wait for a response before using the response to develop the learning process. Don't ask a question and then answer the question yourself! The following pedagogical strategy can help in developing deep learning.

1. Think carefully about a clear question and write the question out.
2. Divide the children into groups to work on answering the question.
3. Get feedback from the children.
4. Write up the best ideas.
5. 'Top up' the children's understanding of the key concepts that are being explored.
6. Summarize the main learning goals.

This pedagogical strategy ought to be based on a 'problem centred approach'. As opposed to teaching 'content', the learners ought to be given a challenge and then be expected to study this content in order to provide a solution to the problem. A way of facilitating this form of pedagogy is to adopt a 'case-study approach'. If you give the learners a 'case study' (or scenario) with questions or other tasks to give the topic practical relevance, this can help the children to think 'holistically'. It is also important to ensure that tasks are set in order to develop 'creative responses' from the children. If children are encouraged to design leaflets, and posters and then in turn enabled to present this content, their sense of deep learning is more likely to be developed.

Try to make sure that you ask 'higher order questions' from Bloom's Taxonomy as opposed to the lower order (or 'jabberwocky') questions. This in turn requires the children to become involved with the 'analysis, synthesis and evaluation' of learning concepts. Make sure that your lessons are structured around 'questions' rather than 'answers' so that curiosity becomes part of the pedagogical process. Questions like 'why do trees lose their leaves in winter?' or 'why is chocolate so lovely?' develop the pedagogical process because your learners are telling you answers as opposed to you telling them the answers! Deep learning involves the critical analysis of new ideas. These ideas ought to be linked to previously known concepts and principles. This in turn helps to develop understanding and long-term retention of concepts so that the learning process can be used for problem solving in unfamiliar contexts. Haughton (2004) states that deep learning promotes understanding and allows the learning process to be applied to a variety of contexts. In contrast, surface learning is the tacit acceptance that information is 'isolated' and not connected to a profound level of learning. The learning process becomes characterized by a superficial retention of material and there is no promotion of understanding or long-term retention of knowledge and information.

Good classroom communication skills

Teaching is generally considered as only 50 per cent knowledge and 50 per cent interpersonal or communication skills. For a teacher in early years, it is not just important to give a quality lesson but it is just as important that the lesson is communicated effectively. Most experienced teachers would agree that communication skills for teachers are just as important as the in-depth knowledge of a particular subject that is being taught.

Teachers need to be aware of the importance of communication skills in teaching. It is also important to realize that children have different levels of skills and needs. The communication skills of the teacher become essential if creative and effective solutions to the challenges within the learning process are to be found. We need effective communication in pedagogy for a variety of reasons. We may need to modify behaviour by using verbal and non-verbal cues in order to get the required behavioural response. To get 'action' from the children or 'persuade' our learners to do a learning activity, we may need particularly good communication skills. We need to apply communication skills in order to ensure that our learners understand what they are supposed to be doing. The most common forms of communication are the spoken word, the written word, visual images and body language. Communication can be described as being the process of sending and receiving information. If ever the information does not get to the 'sender/receiver', this can be due to 'distortion'.

Non-verbal communication

It is not only what you say in the classroom that is important but also how you say it that can make the difference to your children. Non-verbal messages are an essential component of communication in the teaching process. Teachers should be aware of non-verbal behaviour in the classroom for three major reasons:

1. Awareness of non-verbal behaviour allows you to become more aware of how your children are communicating.
2. You will become a better communicator if you become aware of non-verbal messages.
3. This mode of communication increases the degree of the perceived psychological closeness between the teacher and the learner.

Some major areas of non-verbal behaviours that are important are:

1. *Eye contact.* This is an important channel of interpersonal communication that helps in regulating the flow of communication. It signals interest in others. Eye contact with audiences increases the speakers' credibility. Teachers who make eye contact open the flow of communication and convey interest, concern, warmth and credibility.

2. *Facial expressions.* Smiling is a powerful cue that transmits happiness, friendliness, warmth, liking and affection. If you smile frequently, you will

be perceived as being more likeable, friendly, warm and approachable. Smiling is often contagious and students will react favourably and learn more.

3. *Gestures*. If you fail to use gestures while speaking, you may be perceived as being 'unanimated' in your teaching. A lively and animated teaching style captures the children's attention and makes the material more interesting. This can in turn facilitate learning and provide a bit of entertainment. 'Nods' can also help in communicating positive reinforcement to the children and indicate that you are listening to what they are saying.

4. *Posture and body orientation*. We communicate numerous messages by the way we walk, talk, stand and sit. Standing erect, but not rigid, and leaning slightly forward communicates to the children that you are approachable, respectful and friendly. Furthermore, interpersonal closeness results when you and your students face each other. Speaking with your back turned or looking at the floor or ceiling should be avoided. This can communicate disinterest to your class.

5. *Proximity*. Cultural norms dictate a comfortable distance for interaction with students. You should look for signals of discomfort caused by invading someone's space. Some of these are signs of discomfort include: rocking, leg swinging, tapping and gaze aversion. To counteract this possibility, move around the classroom to increase interaction with your children. Increasing proximity enables you to make better eye contact and increases the opportunities for the children to speak.

6. *Para-linguistics*. This aspect of non-verbal communication includes the vocal elements of tone, pitch, rhythm, timbre, loudness and inflection. For maximum effectiveness in teaching, learn to vary these elements of your voice. If you speak to the children in a 'monotone' voice, your style of teaching may be criticized. The children may learn less and then find that they lose interest in learning.

7. *Humour*. This aspect of pedagogy is sometimes overlooked as a teaching tool. Laughter releases stress and tension for both the teacher and the children. It is important to develop an ability to laugh at yourself and encourage your children to make sure that they are never too serious. This in turn fosters a friendly classroom environment that can help in facilitating learning.

8. *Intelligence*. Not everyone can teach well! You need knowledge of your subjects as this will help in engendering confidence. It is also important to ensure that you help in generating an atmosphere that facilitates learning. To improve your non-verbal skills, you might want to record your speaking on

audio tape. You could then ask a colleague to suggest how you might change your style of delivery. You might also consider watching a recording of your teaching as this can also help you to evaluate your non-verbal skills.

Verbal communication

Verbal communication is one way for people to communicate face-to-face. Some of the key components of verbal communication are sound, words, speaking and language. Oral communication is a process whereby information is transferred from a sender to a receiver usually by a verbal means but visual aids can also support the process. When you communicate face to face, the body language you use alongside the tonality of your voice has a bigger impact than the actual words that you are saying. According to Petty (2009):

- 55 per cent of the impact is determined by your awareness of body language (posture, gesture, eye contact).
- 38 per cent is determined by the tone of your voice.
- 7 per cent is determined by the content of your words during the communication process.

Therefore *how you say it* has a major impact on your learners. You have to capture the attention of the audience and make a connection with them. For example, out of two people saying the same joke, one of them could make the audience laugh with their body language and tone of voice. The second person, however, could use the exact same words but make the audience stare at one another in exasperation.

When you are using oral communication, it is important to make sure that you have visual aids in order to help you to provide more precise information. An electronic teaching board may help to facilitate or enhance the communication process. This aspect of communication can be combined with written words and visual images in order to develop the learning process.

How can we make verbal communication effective?

- Use clear, good pronunciation of words.
- Use simple language that is easy to understand.
- Avoid using jargon unless it is explained.
- Avoid using abbreviations or acronyms unless they have been previously explained.
- Speak to aid understanding and not to impress.

Effective communication skills in education are easily identified by successful learners. Just as any endeavour will not succeed if the leadership is not effective, so the learning process will be affected negatively if the teacher is not communicating properly. Effective communication in education produces children who understand the information and are in turn motivated to learn more and perform well. When the pedagogical process is based on effective communication, children and teachers become more satisfied with the learning process in general.

In teacher training courses, educators often say that the responsibility of the teacher is to communicate in such a way that every child can understand what is happening in the learning process. Although this is true, it must be considered that each child learns differently and at various rates. Communication must be effective in order for learners to succeed, but each child has a different way to process information.

When a teacher communicates effectively, they will be able to have the authority that allows them to avoid confusion and clarify information. Effective communication also gives direction to the learning process. This in turn provides the students with an idea of where they are heading within the pedagogical process. It is when teachers respond to their learners in an effective way that they can in turn communicate knowledge and enthusiasm about their topic. This will in turn generate respect and appreciation of the pedagogical process.

Emancipatory pedagogy

A number of authors draw attention to the importance of 'emancipatory pedagogy' in order to ensure best practice in pedagogy (Archer and Leathwood (2003), Freire (1973, 1985, 1994), Giroux (2000), Mayo (2013) and Torres (1998, 2008)). If the ideas of these authors are developed, 'moral education' is placed at the centre of pedagogy. Critical pedagogy recommends systematic enquiries into teaching and learning in order to develop teaching and learning. It is this attempt to create understandings of pedagogy as well as change that rests at the heart of critical pedagogy. A merit of critical pedagogy is that attention is drawn to the human relationships that are at the centre of pedagogy. Education is understood to be about realizing individual potential in the fullest sense of the word. Moreover, Freire and Freire (1997, p.80) argue that teaching should be based on a pedagogy in which 'all grow'.

> Through dialogue, the-teacher-of-the-students and the student-of-the-teacher cease to exist and a new term emerges: teacher-student with students-teacher. The teacher is no longer the-one-who-teaches, but one who is himself taught in dialogue with the students, who in turn while being taught also teach.

Far from being visualized as a 'tool' for teaching, pedagogy is perceived by Freire (1997) as being a fundamental component of human nature and a sign that an educator has a democratic understanding of human society.

Summary of key points

In this chapter, we have looked at learning theories and their application to education and the classroom. Each learning theory has been discussed in detail showing clear advantages and disadvantages for each strategy. It is hoped you will use the knowledge gained from looking at the learning theories to link to your curriculum and lesson planning. The chapter has also explored how Bloom's 'taxonomies of learning' can be applied to developing learning. The contents of the chapter can be used to help develop differentiated learning outcomes that will challenge your more able learners as well as meet the needs of your less able learners. The final section of the chapter has explored the importance of communication skills. The chapter content emphasizes that non-verbal communication skills are just as important as verbal skills. Teaching is not an impossible profession. It can be argued that teaching, just like learning, is a discipline. This means that it is important to learn from teaching experiences. Reflect on these experiences. Retain what is positive. Amend and adapt what has been less than positive. This is essentially at the centre of the craft of teaching.

Self-assessment questions

Complete the following sentences.

Question 1
Learning is a relatively permanent change in...............................

Question 2
How does advertising work?

Question 3
Who has used operant conditioning on you and what did they get you to do?

Question 4
Behaviourists believe that all behaviour is ....

Question 5
Name a major cognitivist theorist?

Question 6
Name a humanist theorist who has been discussed within this chapter?

Question 7
What is surface learning?

Question 8
State three ways to apply deeper learning strategies in the classroom.

Question 9
What are the fundamental principles of the Montessori, Regio Emilia and the Steiner approaches to teaching and learning?

Moving on

This chapter has introduced learning theories which feature in every aspect of your planning and presentation of teaching. These theories also impact upon how you manage your classroom. The chapter also focuses on the use of surface and deeper learning which you should consider when writing learning outcomes and planning activities for learners. Continue to think about positive communication skills when studying classroom management as you need to develop your own skills and those of your learners.

Further reading

Petty, G. (2009), *Teaching Today*, 4th ed. Cheltenham: Nelson Thornes.

An excellent textbook that is written in an accessible way and makes clear links to applying theory to practice.

Enhancing Best Practice through Professional Skills

Learning outcomes

After reading this chapter you should be able to:

- have an understanding of the Plowden Report of 1967, which considered the notion of integrated children's services;
- recognize the emergence of the concept of 'educare';
- have a shared understanding of professionalism including diversity, meeting individual needs, alongside following ethical procedures such as confidentiality of information;
- understand the development of these professional skills into a key aspect of employability.

Introduction

This chapter aims to develop your understanding of enhancing best practice through professional skills. The Central Advisory Council for Education (CACE) was established in 1944 following the Education Act 1944 which identified a need to remove the inequalities in the education system and provide education for all. It was intended to be an advisory body for the government and existed for twenty years; the Plowden Report was one of the final studies produced by the Council. 'There shall be two Central Advisory Councils for Education, one for England and the other for Wales and Monmouthshire, and it shall be the duty of those Councils to advise the Minister upon such matters connected with educational theory and practice as they think fit, and upon any questions referred to them by him' (The Education Act, 1944). This was taken through parliament by R. A. Butler and introduced a three tier system of education: grammar, secondary modern and comprehensive schools. It also raised the leaving age to fifteen and the impact on early years was that it established the delivery of early years education in sessions. 'The Report of the Plowden Committee on Children and their Primary Schools (Central Advisory Council for Education, 1967) set the pattern of nursery education to the end of the century and beyond' (Maynard and Thomas, 2009, p.118). This resulted in early years education being delivered in sessions and this was not the case in other countries at that time. However, not everyone agreed with the concept, and changes in the system became inevitable. A main theme of the chapter is to consider the impact of the Plowden Report and the underpinning developmental theories that influenced the recommendations. The notion of an integrated children's service goes back to the Plowden Report of 1967 and the chapter will explore how children's services characterized by professional skills and expertise have witnessed education, health and care transform into the concept of educare. The chapter also demonstrates that the concept of educare is not just a deficit model; it is a positive and professional approach to early years, encouraging the professional on a reflexive journey that should enhance and develop professional skills. Educare, when followed diligently and in a professional manner, has the potential to transform the lives of many, to make a difference – 'joined up solutions' to 'joined up problems'.

The Plowden Report and professional skills

It was considered by some that the selection system within education, which was a result of the 1944 Education Act, was failing the generations. As a result, Sir Edward Boyle, the Conservative education minister in 1963, requested that the Central Advisory Council for Education 'consider primary education in all its aspects, and the transition to secondary education' (Plowden Report (1967)). The committee was comprised of academics, inspectors and practitioners and was chaired by Lady Plowden. They spent three years formulating the report, observing and discussing what could be considered as 'good practice' and then made recommendations for improvements to the primary provision. Labour took power in 1964, so it was Sir Anthony Crosland who, as Secretary of State, received the Report and decided what ought to be instigated.

One of the primary declarations of the Report is that 'At the heart of the educational process lies the child' (Plowden Report, 1967, p.7). The Report is based on the understanding that unless any changes or advancements were in harmony with the child, there would be little chance of them being effective and that crucially, 'underlying all educational questions is the nature of the child' (Plowden Report, 1967, p.7). It was therefore, considered to be of paramount importance to explore children's growth and development in the light of current academic knowledge. Although many factors were considered, the Report only included the ones deemed to be relevant to the given remit.

Among the relevant facts are the early growth of the brain compared with most of the rest of the body; the earlier development of girls compared with boys; the enormously wide variability in physical and intellectual maturity amongst children of the same age, particularly at adolescence, and the tendency nowadays for children to mature physically earlier than they used to.

(Plowden Report, 1967, p.7)

Interestingly, the Report also considered the concept of a developmental sequence which was clarified as the events that were fixed in a recognisable sequence but could be encountered at varying ages. In this, there is a clear reflection of Piaget's theories regarding the 'Stages of Development'. The nature-nurture debate was also acknowledged within the Report although it was assumed that advances in the understanding of genetics and human biology resulted in 'nature' being more important than 'nurture'. The Report therefore focuses on the notion of a developmental age linked to a chrono-logical age – how far the child has advanced towards maturity since birth. There are consistent and persistent references throughout the Report to the child as an individual and a clear acknowledgment of the demands that this places on a practitioner. This leads to a recognition of the requirements for practitioners to be adaptable in their approach and therefore, it follows that in order to facilitate this, the educational system also needs to be as flexible as possible. The Report was influenced by the developmental theory of Piaget. Awareness of Piaget's ideas in turn enhances our professional skills and our employability.

How Piaget helps our professional practice

Piaget (1896–1980) was a biologist. His work on the development of children has had a tremendous impact on our understanding of the growth and devel-opment of children. Though Piaget's work is not without critics (for example Malim and Birch (1998)), his thinking on children and how they grow and learn has had significant impact on the way we understand children's develop-ment. Piaget rejected the idea that children were little adults, that they were just adults in formation. Instead, he identified what he considered were stages of development based on the idea that our knowledge about the world grows over time with experience.

Piaget – stages of development

Piaget questioned the purpose of education – whether it was to teach children things we already know or whether it was to allow them to develop creative, innovative and enquiring minds. Piaget rejected the idea of children as little adults and began to focus on studying their thinking and reasoning patterns. He observed that children constructed their own knowledge based on their experiences and that they learnt many things without the intervention of another person. He also noted that children are intrinsically motivated to learn, they do not require a reward system to entice them to learn. Their motivation is 'curiosity'. Piaget identified learning through 'schemata' or 'schemas'. The child organizes and makes sense of their experiences and observations. Piaget saw these as the building blocks of knowledge.

Stages of learning

Some of Piaget's key terminology is also explained in Chapter 6 of this book. To complement Chapter 6, the following key themes of Piaget's work are subsequently outlined:

'Assimilation' – the child uses previous knowledge to make sense of a new experience. The child translates the new information into something they can understand. Assimilation is building up of information. For example, a child can see a picture of a dog and then when they see a real dog they can identify what it is. Likewise, a child can see a new breed of dog and still identify it as a dog.

A child might understand a tree as being green and having a trunk and leaves. This information can slowly expand – the child will come to realize that although the leaves fall from trees in the autumn, not all trees will lose their leaves, that trees can have different names and still be a tree, that trees are used within the celebration of Christmas that some trees bear fruit and so on.

'Accommodation' – old schemas are adjusted or new ones created to make sense of new experiences or observations. The child adapts current knowledge as a response to a new experience. As an example, a child might see a zebra and assimilate this as a horse – perhaps even a horse with stripes – since it looks similar and has four legs. As the process continues the child eventually learns that the creature is a zebra and the information is accommodated.

'Equilibration' – this is a balance between assimilation and accommodation to create a stable understanding. This can move learning onwards but it is not a steady progression. For example, a child is processing most information through a process of assimilation but then new information comes along that does not fit – it needs accommodating. Disequilibrium is that moment of imbalance or frustration when the child seeks to restore the balance by assimilating the new information.

Stages of cognitive development

Piaget observed that children moved through four stages of development and that they followed these in a precise order. He defined these as the sensorimotor stage, the pre-operational stage, concrete operational stage and the formal operational stage.

Stage of development	Age	Characteristics
Sensorimotor stage Limited to motor reflexes at birth but these develop as the child builds upon these reflexes. They generalize their behaviours to a wider range of situations. They co-ordinate to an increasingly lengthier and more sophisticated chain of behaviour.	0–2 years	The child is learning by looking, touching, sucking. There is some understanding of cause and effect relationships. An understanding of object permanence at around 9 months. Acquiring knowledge through sensory experiences and manipulation of objects. The child can be egocentric – the inability to see the world from another's point of view.
Pre-operational stage Children begin to acquire representational skills, mental imagery and a more sophisticated language. Egocentric – the child views the world from their own perspective.	2–7 years	The child uses language and symbols including letters and numbers. Evidence of egocentric behaviour. Beginning to use conversation (This would mark the end of this stage and the beginning of the concrete stage of development.) Can learn through pretend play but still tends to consider only their own point of view. Can use one object to represent another.
Concrete operational stage Children are able to consider a viewpoint other than their own. They can consider more than one view point. They understand concrete problems but cannot understand all of the possible options of outcomes.	7–11 years	The child understands conversation Has an understanding of cause and effect Can order things. Understands reversing concepts. Thinking remains concrete at this stage. The child can think with logic but has not yet progressed to abstract or theoretical concepts.
Formal operations Children can think logically and abstractly. They can also reason in an abstract sense.	11+ years	Thinking becomes abstract as well. The child can display logic, can compare, can deduce things and can classify information. There is also an increase in logic using deductive reasoning and can consider abstract ideas.

Reviews of the Piagetian stages of development suggest that not every child will reach the 'Formal Operative' stage. Moreover, there is debate as to whether all children follow this rigid progression of development in the order suggested and at the ages set out. It is now thought that not every child reaches the formal operation stage. Developmental psychologists also debate whether children do go through the stages in the way that Piaget postulated. Despite the ongoing debate about the stages of development outlined within Piaget's theory, his theory of cognitive development has had a tremendous influence on early years education. This helps our professional practice and enhances our employability.

Critiques of Piagetian theory

There are critiques of the work of Piaget (for example Malim and Birch (1998)). The criticism here complements the work in Chapter 6. Piaget appears to be more interested in the individual child and the stages of cognitive development – he considered that there were certain things common to all children at a certain level of development. This is applying a concept known as the 'epistemic subject'. However, in considering the stages as universal and applicable to all children, he did not consider the social setting and the cultural implications of this. Vygotsky argued that this was crucial to the child's progression.

In addition, Piaget conducted his observations alone rather than with another researcher and these were principally of his own children. This, therefore, represents a bias and results in a subjective interpretation of data. There are also limitations to Piaget's studies in terms of culture and again it is difficult to apply the results universally. Children involved in his observational research were from the same socio-economic group which again makes it difficult to apply the findings as a general theory. There is also criticism that some of the tasks that Piaget used were difficult to follow, that he underestimated the importance of language to his tasks. Therefore, this again imposes limitations on the results. Vygotsky, while still deemed a constructivist, considered that the social world played a primary role in cognitive development. Indeed, he is referred to as a 'social constructivist'. Language is considered to be an essential component of learning and child development. An emphasis is placed on social and cultural influences on learning. Vygotsky also formulated the idea of a ZPD (or individual potential). This has had a significant impact on educational practice. The educator is responsible for helping to realize each child's inner potential. In Piaget's theory, the teacher has a more limited role whereas

Vygotsky, in emphasizing linguistic and social factors, places more importance on the role of the teacher. The teacher is seen as a guide and facilitator rather than as someone who dispenses knowledge. A nurturing relationship of working in partnership is therefore envisaged.

Reflective Activity 4.1

Does the work of Piaget support the idea of working in partnership?

Feedback

You could argue that Piaget's work is interpreted as drawing attention to the cognitive development of individual children. This may be interpreted as going against the idea of working together in partnership, in that learning could be perceived as 'isolated' since the emphasis is placed on the individual child. The work of Vygotsky draws more attention to the social experience of learning. This notion of learning appears to be more supportive of a philosophy of partnership.

Behaviourist learning

An alternate approach can be seen with the ideas within behaviourism. In Chapter 6, we will see how behaviourism forms part of the holistic way of working with children and families. Behaviourism considers observable behaviour rather than the internalized concept of schemas. The focus is on achieving a change through repetition of an action and rewards for positive behaviour and withdrawal of rewards when there is a non-desirable outcome. This is known as 'operant conditioning', a concept developed by Skinner and the reinforcement of the behaviour needed to be immediate. In settings, this would manifest itself as praise for success and correction of poor behaviour.

The stages of development are also challenged in that they do not allow for any influence from the environment particularly in the formal stage of development. The idea that children will automatically move through the stages of development is also disputed and the age at which children can progress – the stages – is questioned. Again, the universality of this approach, that the theory based on such a limited experimental basis could be considered appropriate for all notwithstanding class, culture or social background, can be questioned.

Undoubtedly though, Piaget has had a great impact on the conception of children's learning and development. His influence on educare is very evident today.

Piaget's impact on education

While Piaget did not relate his work explicitly to education, the features of his theory have been related to teaching and learning. Significantly, the review of education in England and Wales that led to The Plowden Report (1967) was strongly based on the theories developed by Piaget and approached education within stages of development. Children were perceived as 'active learners'. This concept was key to the formation of the curriculum. The role of the teacher was as a facilitator rather than a didactic educator. Following Piagetian Theory, the child would not be expected to have achieved certain concepts until they were at the appropriate stage of development. The practitioner's role evolved into one of a 'facilitator of learning' rather than a teacher or bringer of knowledge. The focus of delivery was on the process rather than just seeking the answer. The child was encouraged to investigate, to discover and to be the means to gaining and extending their own knowledge. The ideas of Vygotsky are evident in that the practitioner is a significant other and can guide and support the child at appropriate moments (ZPD). The Plowden Report in encouraging group work, facilitating investigation and generally promoting the idea of learning by discovery was in fact using the concept of the practitioner as facilitator as a central principle to professional practice. This also extended to peer-support and learning and setting challenging tasks so that a child could make progress.

The Plowden Report (1967) followed several central themes:

- Individual Learning.
- Learning by discovery.
- Using the environment effectively.
- The focus upon play as a key to children's learning and development.
- The importance of evaluating a child's progress.
- The notion that not everything that was valuable could be measured.

Early years education and the Plowden Report

The Plowden Report 'set the pattern of nursery education to the end of the century and beyond' (Maynard and Thomas, 2009, p.118). This was primarily delivered in sessions lasting two and half hours either in the morning or in the afternoon and had the 'perverse effect of ending most existing full-time nursery provision' (Maynard and Thomas, 2009, p.118). This made it difficult for mothers returning to work to access nursery education. The focus of part of the debate became whether nursery education was about enabling mothers to work or providing a happy, caring and educational environment that would allow children to develop and learn. This is a debate that continues till today.

Nature-nurture debate

The debate centres on whether learning and development is a result of inherited genes or experience or a combination of the two. How far are behaviours innate and how far they are learned? This is a focus for many studies and an ongoing discussion. John Locke (1632–1704) a philosopher in the seventeenth century, considered that the mind was a 'tabula rasa' or 'blank slate'. Children were empty vessels to be filled with knowledge and understanding; they were not limited by their innate capacity to learn. However, to consider all learning and development as a product of the environment is no longer considered to be tenable. If this is the case, then what do young children use to effectively make sense of their surroundings and experiences?

Nevertheless, children's earliest experiences do impact upon their learning and development and as such can make a huge difference but, very importantly, later intervention can also make a difference. This was evidenced in the Effective Provision of Pre-school Education (EPPE) research project which concluded that 'High Quality Early Childhood Education (ECE) can be a strong equalizer for the most disadvantaged children. While all children benefit from high quality ECE, some only get it through pre-school provision rather than in the home' (Siraj-Blatchford and Sylva, 2004 cited in Maynard and Thomas, 2009, p.153).

Interpretations of good practice in early years

In the opening statements of the Plowden Report (1967), the philosophy of child-centred education was declared. 'At the heart of the Educational Process lies the child. No advances in policy, no acquisitions of new equipment have their desired effect unless they are in harmony with the nature of the child, unless they are fundamentally acceptable to him' (Plowden Report, 1967, p.7).

Furthermore, the Report recognized the importance of understanding early years learning and development. 'Knowledge in the manner in which children develop, therefore, is of prime importance, both in avoiding educationally harmful practices and in introducing effective ones' (Plowden Report, 1967, p.7). This reinforces the key aim of educating the early years workforce, that knowledge of children's learning and development was a key area of 'good practice'.

Critics of the Plowden Report (1967) consider some of the aims to be unrealistic. Kogan (1987) develops a 'reductionist critique' of the Report. It is argued that the approach of the Report reduces the delivery of education to simply allowing the child to flourish. Another key concern is that the 'emphasis placed on the individual child is unrealistic'. It is not possible for teachers to cater for 30 individuals each pursuing their own development and at the same time ensure a worthwhile common core education was available to all! (Kogan, 1987, p.6).

The emergence of the key concept of educare for professional practice

The importance of early years was recognized in policy and approach when in 1998 the government brought out a National Childcare Strategy Green Paper: Meeting the Childcare Challenge (1998). With this came the concept of educare – the notion that education and care of the child in the early stages of development and beyond were clearly linked. The term 'early years' also came into being. With the recognition of the links between education and care came the concept of the 'joined-up' approach to childcare in early years. As noted by Maynard and Thomas (2009, p.121), 'childcare' – one word – was used in documentation replacing 'day care' and was distinctly different to the term 'child care' – two words – which referred to substitute care for children. In addition to the change in approach, there was also greater access to early years education.

Reflective Activity 4.2

What are the benefits of educare?

Feedback

There are many benefits to having what is referred to by Tony Blair as 'joined-up solutions to joined-up problems'. As opposed to having separate departments of 'health', 'education' and 'care', the idea of educare is based on principles of cooperation and working together. We can argue that this is a more effective way of working to meet the needs of children and families. Resources are combined together and cooperation is encouraged in order to meet the needs of children and families. It is also important to note that the Laming Report (2003) that led to the emergence of integrated services was commissioned as a response to the Victoria Climbié case.

Victoria Climbié

Victoria Climbié was eight years old when she died as a result of sustained abuse at the hands of her carers – her great aunt and her aunt's boyfriend. What was most worrying in terms of contributing factors to the case was the fact that so many different professional services were involved with the case before the final tragic outcome. Despite the involvement of these professionals, they failed to progress any further understanding of the child's circumstances and crucially did not share the information to produce a coherent whole that had the potential to alert the professionals and stimulate some action. While Victoria Climbié was clearly a 'child at risk', this was overlooked and following her death, the Laming Report (2003) was commissioned to try to ascertain why and how this had occurred.

One of the key recommendations of the Report was the integration of the various services for children – a sharing of information. This was to be enacted for all children – not just those considered to be at risk. The main means to implement this was through the Every Child Matters agenda. The aims of the proposals contained within Every Child Matters were clearly stated by Tony Blair, the prime minister at that time, within the document.

> Every inquiry has brought forward proposals for change and improvement to the child protection system. There have been reforms. Things have got better for many. But the fact that a child like Victoria Climbié can still suffer almost

unimaginable cruelty to the point of eventually losing her young life shows that things are still very far from right. More can and must be done.

Responding to the inquiry headed by Lord Laming into Victoria Climbié's death, we are proposing here a range of measures to reform and improve children's care – crucially, for the first time ever requiring local authorities to bring together in one place under one person services for children, and at the same time suggesting real changes in the way those we ask to do this work carry out their tasks on our and our children's behalf. For children for whom action by the authorities has reduced the risk they face, we want to go further: we want to maximise the opportunities open to them – to improve their life chances, to change the odds in their favour.

(Blair, Every Child Matters, 2003, Forward p.1)

The Green Paper acknowledged the importance of reviewing the past failings. Opportunities to protect Victoria Climbié had been missed on twelve occasions and the Laming Report (2003) clearly identified that the social services, the police and the NHS had failed to do the basic things in order to protect her. It also cited previous cases including Maria Colwell and Jasmine Beckford, Lauren Wright and Ainlee Walker identifying the common thread which led to failure to intervene early enough as being 'poor co-ordination; a failure to share information; the absence of anyone with a strong sense of accountability; and frontline workers trying to cope with staff vacancies, poor management and a lack of effective training' (Every Child Matters, 2003, p.5).

The idea that this was not intended simply as a deficit model aimed at supporting vulnerable children was, however, also clearly stated. The intent was to support all children and maximize their potential and opportunity. 'As Lord Laming's recommendations made clear, child protection cannot be separated from policies to improve children's lives as a whole' (Every Child Matters, 2003, p.5).

Every Child Matters (2003) and professional practice

The Every Child Matters (2003) policy framework documentation was also introduced as an attempt to provide integrated children's services. This was a key initiative in early years. It outlined five outcomes.

- Stay Safe
- Healthy

- Enjoy and Achieve
- Economic Well-Being
- Positive Contribution

Crucially, what was recognized as a key element was the concept of the integrated (Table 4.1) approach. The Every Child Matters (2003) Green Paper was followed by Every Child Matters: Change for Children (2004) and the Children Act of 2004. It confirmed the five outcomes and clearly stated that the aims were for all children. The main focus was identified as early intervention, a shared sense of responsibility, information sharing and integrated front line services. The emphasis was recognized as aiming to enable each child to fulfil their potential. The means to achieve this was through cooperation between government agencies, schools and health as well as with the voluntary sector and community links. These goals were intended to be a positive approach for the child's learning and development rather than simply a deficit model. The 2010 elections brought in a coalition government and changes began to happen almost immediately. The language and terminology changed – Every Child Matters and the five outcomes being replaced by 'Help Children Achieve More' (December, 2010).

Table 4.1 Every Child Matters (2003), pp.6–7

Five outcomes and aims	
• Stay Safe	enjoying good physical and mental health and living a healthy lifestyle.
• Healthy	being protected from harm and neglect.
• Enjoy and Achieve	getting the most out of life and developing the skills for adulthood.
• Economic Well-Being	being involved with the community and society and not engaging in anti-social or offending behaviour.
• Positive Contribution	not being prevented by economic disadvantage from achieving their full potential in life.

Ten Year Childcare Strategy (2004) and the Childcare Act (2006)

The Ten Year Strategy (2004) outlined some key commitments for early years and, as such, impacted on the employability demands placed upon the early years professionals. It was based on the five learning outcomes set out in Every Child Matters (2003). The strategy was based on considering how children's centres can facilitate children's growth and development. The focus was on 'educare' – the strategy outlining the need for centres to provide a range of services that offered advice and support to parents and carers. This was a recognition of the integration of childcare and early years learning and development, health services, outreach work, parental support and advice for disadvantaged parents. It considered the need for qualification standards to be maintained within the profession for those engaged in early years provision, and this provision was deemed an entitlement. The Childcare Act (2006) aimed to improve childcare in early years partly through giving access to greater provision.

Help Children Achieve More (2010) and professional practice

As an integral part of 'Help Children Achieve More' (2010), the document sets out the basic skills and knowledge needed by practitioners:

- Effective communication and engagement with children, young people and families.
- Child and young person development.
- Safeguarding and promoting the welfare of the child.
- Supporting transitions.
- Multi-agency working.
- Sharing information.

Clearly, the agenda supports the concept of educare in placing an emphasis on multi-agency working and sharing of information in promoting the welfare of the child. In order to meet these needs, the practitioner has to take a more holistic approach; and the need to work with other disciplines is a key theme within the document. The concept underlines the concept of educare. This recognizes the professionalism and the significance of the role of the different support services but importantly, in recognizing the importance of the holistic needs of the child, it also emphasizes the importance of different services working together. Educare considers the unique child and aims to support the learning and development of the child. It is not intended to be a deficit model or approach, rather a pro-active acknowledgement that working together is to the benefit of the child regardless of what the specific needs tend to be. Supporting the learning and development of the child is best achieved by an integrated approach from the various services of education, health and social care. This in turn has impacted on practitioners who need to be part of an extended team in ensuring the best provision for each child. While not intended that the practitioner should be qualified or able to deal with every eventuality on a personal basis in caring for the well-being of those in their charge, there is a greater need to share information in order to more effectively support the child. In all this, however, there remains the ethical consideration of the confidentiality of the information. It is shared with those who need to be aware of the issues and circumstances but confidentiality is preserved. In delivering an effective educare approach, the practitioner also needs to have a shared understanding of the diversity of needs as well as a professional respect for the ethical procedures and concerns including recognizing the confidentiality of information. The focus on the unique child evident in the Plowden Report (1967) and subsequent initiatives and legislation is central to the educare approach.

A shared understanding of professionalism

The emphasis on improving standards of provision in early years and the importance of an integrated service approach acknowledged in educare has also resulted in a drive to improve the education and training of professionals in the field of early years provision. The important recognition was that quality childcare was key to the effective delivery of the standards and aims of early years provision. Indeed, the development of specific named degrees in Early Childhood Studies is a very clear reflection of this approach. The degree programmes tend to offer a greater understanding of social policy, ethics, safeguarding and the pedagogy of the professional practitioner. These topics underpin a shared understanding needed by the practitioner in order to facilitate the learning and development of the child and the ability to meet the needs and purpose of the educare agenda.

The focus of the 'unique child' evident in the Plowden Report (1967) and subsequent frameworks, initiatives and legislation is central to the educare approach. 'The educational component of early years provision has the potential to transform a child's life and set them on a positive learning trajectory for life' (Maynard and Thomas, 2009, p.149). The concerns for the notion of introducing the concept of educare – the joined-up approach to professional practice in early years has been driven by a number of cases where the child's health, welfare and education have been overlooked with tragic consequences. The Victoria Climbié case, which resulted in the commissioning of the Laming Report (2003) that recommended the integration of the services and a sharing of information, has been followed by other cases that have resulted in a child's death as a result of abuse or neglect. Recent cases in 2013 include those of Keanu Williams in Birmingham, Hamzah Khan in Bradford and Daniel Pelka in Coventry. There have been calls to review the remit of serious case reviews so that they focus on the question of why it happened rather than just considering what happened in a particular case. In asking why this happened, there emerges an opportunity for the professionals to learn. There is also a move away from a 'blame culture'. However, the case review for the Daniel Pelka case did highlight that one of the main concerns was that practitioners had not dared to 'think the unthinkable'. The report endeavoured not to blame an individual or a single agency but considered that the professionals were too optimistic about what they saw and needed to have a more enquiring mind.

Overall, however, these responses do seem to suggest that there is still a tendency to apportion 'blame' and that it lies at the local level – a failure within a specific local authority, a lack of communication relating to a specific case, a failure relating to a lack of professionalism and a failure to challenge and bring about change. Successive governments have been mainly focused on what they have perceived as a lack of professional skills and inherent in this argument, is the idea that with further training, all can be remedied and cases like these need not occur again. However, it is rather disingenuous to reduce these complex arguments to such a simplistic answer. While we strive as a society to try to prevent such tragic reoccurrences, surely training alone cannot provide the answers. Governments are of course reluctant to acknowledge this because of the potential costs involved, yet an increase in funding could, for instance, have an immediate impact on the number of cases a social worker would have to manage at the same time.

As a society, however, it is our duty to speak out for children, to give them a voice. They are amongst the most vulnerable members of our society and are often in positions that could leave them vulnerable to harm. The enclosed family unit, while a place of security and love for many children, can also form a barrier to outsiders, leaving the child in a potentially defenceless position. Part of the professionalism of the practitioner is to speak out for the children – to give them a voice.

The Common Assessment Framework (CAF)

The aims of the Help Children Achieve More (2010) legislation include:

- Multi-agency working.
- The sharing of information.
- Safeguarding and promoting the welfare of the child.

However, the integration in the processes and strategies inherent in the recent legislation extended beyond agencies working together – it involves community and parental involvement. This again has an impact on the professional practice of the practitioner. In order to achieve an integrated policy one of the central mechanisms employed is the Common Assessment Framework (CAF). It is a standardized approach used by practitioners to assess children's additional needs and considers how they should be addressed. Crucially it is an integrated approach that enables information about the child to be shared. The needs of the child are considered holistically and one single record is kept avoiding duplication and presenting a complete picture. The family have a single assessment resulting in a single plan with a single point of contact to work as a nominated person who assumes the role of 'lead professional'. This is usually agreed within the meetings and requires professional skills in terms of communication and co-ordination. The role involves building trust with the child and family. For early years, this necessitates having the skills to communicate with the child in a way that is appropriate to their age and understanding. It also requires the ability and skills to coordinate the delivery of the services.

The process is voluntary, so consent is needed from the families or carers. The CAF process is a request for support services rather than a referral and is intended to consider additional needs for a child. A CAF can be instigated by the family. It is also important to stress that this is not a risk assessment and any safeguarding issue would be subject to a different procedure. The need to share information has to be balanced and the boundaries observed in terms of ethics and safeguarding.

While there are advantages to the collaborative approach including the use of specialist knowledge and avoiding duplication of effort and recording, there are concerns that the number of services involved in itself can be bewildering. The practitioner in early years, as part of the front line of services, can be a key link between the child, parent and services.

The collaborative approach can also be criticized in that no single agency has the whole picture – the information might well be gathered but no single source has the whole picture. The recent cases already cited, Keanu Williams, Hamzah Khan and Daniel Pelka, highlight some of these issues where the lack of effective integration is a crucial element of the tragic outcome which suggests that the co-ordinated strategy still needs some improvement to be more effective.

Effective communication and engagement with children, young people and families

Effective communication and engagement with children, young people and families is a key area of the document 'Help Children Achieve More' (2010). The knowledge and understanding of how to work towards this goal through professional skills effectively enhances best practice. This includes an understanding of a child-centred approach and enabling environments, an awareness of the child's voice, parents as partners, an appreciation of diversity and inclusivity and, of course, the knowledge of children's learning and development including language skills for early years.

The child-centred approach, play and enabling environments

Plowden considered the child-centred view that children learn best when they pursue self-initiated activities, and within the Report this was referred to as 'discovery learning'. 'The sense of personal discovery influences the sense of the child's experience, the vividness of his memory and the probability of effective transfer of learning' (The Plowden Report, 1967, p.201). Not all can be achieved by 'discovery learning' and Plowden recognizes that the skilled practitioner will encourage children in their discovery and ask leading questions. In following their own interests and pursuits, the child 'learns how to learn' – 'The child is the agent of his own learning' (Plowden, 1967, p.194). A practitioner needs to be confident in encouraging child-initiated learning and they also need to provide an enabling environment.

Play is central to early learning and can be 'both purposeful and concentrated or trivial and apparently lacking in purpose, and it can be characterized by focused, motivated and creative behaviour or seemingly aimless "pottering"' (Waller and Swann, 2009, p.41). The central role of play in the early years curriculum is still debated but remains difficult to define which in turn contributes to the argument about its validity and direct contribution to children's learning and development. McInnes et al. (2013) also identify this as problematic and furthermore recognize that while practitioners say they understand the importance of play, they may not seem to act upon this belief. There can be 'a mismatch between what practitioners believe and say about play and their practice' (McInnes et al., 2013, p.271). Interestingly, the Tickell Report also identified this as a concern in that 'there is confusion about what learning through play actually means' (Tickell, 2011, p.28). It does however remain central to the curriculum and an understanding of its importance and effective delivery and support is a key skill for the effective practitioner. 'Within early childhood education, play is central to teaching and learning but it is considered difficult to define. Play may be most beneficial when it is considered as an approach to a task, and based on a definition of play from the child's perspective' (McInnes et al., 2013, p.268).

Indeed, play is enshrined in the United Nations Convention on the Rights of the Child under 'Article 31: (leisure, play and culture). Every child has the right to relax, play and take part in a wide range of cultural and artistic activities' (United Nations Convention on the Rights of the Child, 1989).

It is this pedagogy of play that epitomizes how best practice can be enhanced through professional skills. The emergence of play as a means to engage children in their own learning, understanding and development means the practitioner has to appreciate how to direct and enable the environment in order for the learning opportunities to be available. This is also embedded in the Development Matters in the Early Years Foundation Stage Document (EYFS) 2012. 'The ways in which the child engages with other people and their environment – playing and exploring, active learning, and creating and thinking critically – underpin learning and development across all areas and support the child to remain an effective learner' (EYFS, 2012, p.4). The document considers the development in age range, echoing the progressive stages of development considered by Piaget. However, interestingly, throughout the document there is a warning not to follow the stages rigidly – they are a guide, not a fixed boundary. Children develop at their own rates and in their own way. The development statements and their order should not be taken as necessary steps for individual children. They should not be used as checklists. 'The age/stage bands overlap because these are not fixed boundaries but suggest a typical range of development' (EYFS, 2012). The document is set out in four themes which underpin the guidance: A Unique Child, Positive Relationships, Enabling Environments and Learning and Development.

Considering the practice element of this overview, the early years specialist can offer a (Table 4.2) number of skills in order to promote and share good practice in supporting the development and learning of the child. These are the key skills and when delivered positively and well they can make such a difference for the child. In these terms then the practitioner can enhance their best practice through these professional skills. There is guidance throughout the document outlining examples of practice opportunities for the adult in order to promote the positive relationships and what they could provide in terms of an enabling environment. This recognizes the impact good practice can have on the world of the child.

Recent emphasis on play in early years has also seen the emergence of outdoor play – the realization that the outdoors is another learning environment that can be harnessed and linked effectively to health and well-being. However, the outdoors can offer great opportunities than simply a recognition that being outside is a healthy environment – it is also a unique environment, dynamic and offering multi-sensory experiences, one that has the potential to be at the command of the young. They can use the outdoors to expand, extend and enhance their learning, use trial and error, construct meanings and investigate their own theories. In addition, they learn to take acceptable risks, to evaluate situations and become increasingly skilled at playing safely. The opportunity of independence offered by outdoor play can raise a child's self-esteem as well as broadening their learning experience and development. The skilled practitioner recognizes the opportunities offered by taking the classroom outdoors.

Table 4.2 (EYFS, 2012, p. 2)

Themes	A unique child	Positive relationships	Enabling environments	Learning and development
Principles	Every child is a unique child who is constantly learning and can be resilient, capable, confident and self-assured.	Children learn to be strong and independent through positive relationships.	Children learn and develop well in enabling environments, in which their experiences respond to their individual needs and there is a strong partnership between practitioners and parents and carers.	Children develop and learn in different ways. The framework covers the education and care of all children in early years provision, including children with special educational needs and disabilities.
Practice	Practitioners • understand and observe each child's development and learning, assess progress, plan for next steps • support babies and children to develop a positive sense of their own identity and culture • identify any need for additional support • keep children safe • value and respect all children and families equally	Positive relationships are • warm and loving, and foster a sense of belonging • sensitive and responsive to the child's needs, feelings and interests • supportive of the child's own efforts and independence • consistent in setting clear Boundaries • stimulating • built on key person relationships in early years settings	Enabling Environments • value all people • value learning They offer • stimulating resources, relevant to all the children's cultures and communities • rich learning opportunities through play and playful teaching • support for children to take risks and explore	Practitioners teach children by ensuring challenging, playful opportunities across the prime and specific areas of learning and development. They foster the characteristics of effective early learning • playing and exploring • active learning • creating and thinking critically

Bronfenbrenner – the ecology of human development and professional practice

Bronfenbrenner (1979) argues that the practitioner is a key part of the learning environment for the child – a key figure in the child's relationships. Bronfenbrenner considers that development is a result of relationships between people and their environment. He developed 'The Ecological Systems Theory' and expanded this by considering the child within the social context of the environment. The implication is that the child's development is influenced by the immediate and wider environments. Bronfenbrenner's work regards children and child development in a complex and intricate way. Children and childhood is recognized as being experienced differently by different children in different societies. While many biological factors remain similar, the social experience and social factors impact on the social world of the child. Bronfenbrenner conceives an ecological model that places the child at the centre of his theory. Within this theory is the acknowledgement that the social environment influences and contributes to the child's learning and development. The quality of the experiences and interactions have important implications for the child. There are four layers embedded in the theory – the 'Microsystem', the 'Mesosystem', the 'Exosystem' and the 'Macrosystem'.

'The Microsystem': The relationships of direct contact with the child. These include the family but also the nursery or childcare settings, the school, peer groups and the neighbourhood. The family is regarded as being the most influential and durable factor influencing the child.

'The Mesosystem': The connection between relationships of the child's microsystem. This is a link between the layers. This includes the relationship between the practitioners in the setting and the family. It also includes the relationship between the child's peers and the family.

'The Exosystem': Environments where the child does not have direct contact such as the parental workplace or the political environment that dictates an economic agenda such as funding in early years.

'The Macrosystem': The cultural context including the political culture, the economic culture and other sub-cultures. This influences how the child is raised. It provides the values, customs and beliefs by which a child grows and influences how a child is raised.

Bronfenbrenner added a further layer, 'The Chronosystem', to recognize that children interact with their environment differently at different times of their lives. 'As transitions and chronological events occur, the child is developing not just physically and cognitively but emotionally, as well' (Gray and MacBlain, 2012, p.97).

While these layers are complex and bi-directional, they do reinforce the importance of the individual child. This, in turn, connects with the concept of the child as 'unique'. The role of the practitioner and the professional skills are therefore very important in that it follows that the experiences and interactions within the settings are part of the social world of the child and therefore of paramount importance to the child's learning and development. The relationship within the 'Mesosystem', as defined by Bronfenbrenner, highlights the link between the family and the practitioner and recognizes the importance of this area of practice.

Parents as partners and professional practice

One of the stated key aims of the Early Years Foundation Stage document is to strengthen partnerships between parents and professionals. 'Parents are children's first and most enduring educators. When parents and practitioners work together in early years settings, the results have a positive impact on children's development and learning' (EYFS, 2003, p.2).

There have been a number of government initiatives that reinforce this including 'The Impact of Parental Involvement on Children's Education' (2009 – online) in which the key findings state that 'Parental involvement in children's education from an early age has a significant effect on educational achievement, and continues to do so into adolescence and adulthood' (The Impact of Parental Involvement on Children's Education, 2009 – online). It also concluded that 'Family learning can also provide a range of benefits for parents and children including improvements in reading, writing and numeracy as well as greater parental confidence in helping their child at home' (The Impact of Parental Involvement on Children's Education, 2009 – online). For it to be maintained, effective strategies need to be put in place to facilitate communication and contact with parents and carers.

The implications in embracing this pedagogy and recognizing the links with best practice are significant. It is important to ensure that the relationship of the practitioner and the child are as positive as possible. There is also the need to create an environment that welcomes and nurtures families. In order to have a sense of partnership, there needs to be good communication and it needs to be multi-directional. The team needs to communicate with each other as well as with the parents. The dangers of not working in partnership are only too evident in the tragic child death cases. The serious case-study reports on these cases tend to show that failure to communicate has contributed to the failure to protect the child. Sometimes, however, there has been recognition that there has been over-collusion between parents and professionals and that the child's voice has been overlooked. The professionals have failed to look after the vulnerable. Occasionally, as in the case of Ainlee Walker in 2002, the professionals were frightened by parental aggression – they did not challenge when they should have done. However, this is the deficit model and from this emerged the awareness that there are positive outcomes for children's learning and development in supporting and engaging with parents. This should be founded on a base of mutual respect and a recognition and acceptance that parents can bring much to the agenda as they have the greatest knowledge of their own children. They can support and enhance the best practice within the settings. Children learn to be independent through the positive relationships that are established. The partnership between parents and professionals is essential to the well-being of the child and best practice is enhanced through this positive connection. However, as Neaum argues,

> Partnership suggests a two-way, dynamic relationship in which both partners bring a range of knowledge and skills to a situation in order to understand an issue or solve a problem…. It is argued that the interventions are not, in practice, a partnership approach but are in fact based on a particular understanding of what it means to be a 'good parent' and the aim is to encourage parents to adopt this style of parenting.
>
> (Neaum, 2010, pp.110–111)

The question is – who should define 'good parenting'? Is there only one way to be a 'good parent'? Clearly there are many views of what it means to be a 'good parent' and as each child is unique, parenting cannot remain the same for all nor can it attempt to adopt a 'best fit' approach. This has particular relevance to the understanding of the parental role and the formation of professional relationships in an increasingly diverse society. The Early Years Foundation Stage Document notes that: 'Sometimes practitioners assume that their own way of being a parent, a family member or relating to children is the only right way to do things, but effective parenting can take many different forms' (EYFS Parents as Partners, 2007, p.1). The Tickell Review (2011) was an independent re-examination of the EYFS document and recommended changes to the EYFS document in order to strengthen the partnership between parents and professionals. It was recognized that this was important to the well-being and learning and development of the child. It acknowledged that there was good practice but it needed to be 'spread more widely and to become more consistent' (Tickell, 2011, p.10). The reviewed document was aimed at making this more accessible to 'help promote closer collaboration between parents and carers and practitioners' (Tickell, 2011, p.10).

The social view – inclusivity and diversity

Society is diverse and inclusive practice recognizes and celebrates that diversity. The concern is that practitioners can impose their vision of good-parenting upon others possibly without realizing the rationale or sometimes because they are unable or unwilling to acknowledge that good parenting can take different forms. 'There are multiple and diverse childhoods and, in order to study childhood, one has to consider a range of perspectives' (Waller, 2009, p.5). It is important to remember that inclusion is not about treating everyone in the same way – an even-handed approach – it is about meeting the needs of the child. The good, knowledgeable practitioner will recognize barriers to a child's learning and development and the skill is in then trying to meet those needs so that every child can reach their full potential. The concept of inclusion goes beyond the moral need to include those with disabilities or special educational needs; it is also about cultural inclusion and giving access to all, it is about a sense of belonging. Indeed, it was noted in the EPPE Report that inclusive provision in early years settings was linked to the quality of the staff that worked in them (Sylva et al., 2003).

Enabling environments

This is a key theme of the early years guidance, and within the document there are clear examples of what is envisaged by enabling environments. The learning environment in terms of access to facilities, a language-rich environment, small world areas, role play opportunities, and so on, are some part of this. Another part links with the rationale of outdoor play but it is not solely placed within this environment. Nor is it placed solely within a physical domain. An enabling environment is about establishing open and trusting relationships. It involves responding to the child's needs in terms of language and emotional support, in creating a sustained caring environment in which the child can flourish. A positive relationship with the child is part of providing an environment that enables the child to fully express themselves and begin to develop to their full potential. The skills of the practitioner can enhance this opportunity and the awareness of these opportunities to make a difference are part of best practice. The emergence of the understanding of the reflective practitioner is also incorporated into the best practice envisaged in the EYFS document. To reflect and consider what has worked well and what could be done to improve the learning environment, the learning opportunities and the relationships within early years.

Reflective Activity 4.3

What are the key areas of children's development within an enabling environment?

Feedback

A way of understanding child development is to think of the ways that children develop that are physical, intellectual, emotional and social. This development ought to be enabled by a curriculum that is balanced. Too often, there can be the occurrence of a 'top-heavy' curriculum where intellectual development is regarded as being most important. A balance of physical, intellectual, emotional and social activities ought to be included.

Professional skills for employability

Studying for an Early Childhood Studies Degree or enrolling on Early Years Teacher status already introduces the concept of professional skills. The course will have delivered guidance and information on many areas of practice. Knowledge of legislation is an important factor and there should be a good understanding of the evolution of education and educational practices over time. Key areas of legislation include the Plowden Report (1967), Every Child Matters (2003), Every Child Matters: Time for Change (2004), The Children Act (2004), Ten Year Childcare Strategy (2004), The Childcare Act (2006) and Help Children Achieve More (December, 2010).

A newly qualified practitioner will be able to apply their knowledge and understanding of issues of safeguarding and ethics. They should also be aware of the different initiatives such as Every Child a Talker and Parents as Partners. In addition to this, the student and thereby the practitioner who has followed this route will have other skills which will benefit the employment role. These skills include time management and 'all the skills and qualities of independence and decision-making that employers often look for in their graduates' (Sambell et al., 2010, p.126). Additionally, the greater understanding of children's learning and development and the need for the holistic view of children and early childhood gives a greater awareness and appreciation of the role of practitioner. Knowledge of working with parents and the community, an understanding of the needs of diversity and inclusive practice and an appreciation of the links between society and education are key skills in developing professional practice.

Summary of key points

This chapter has introduced concept of educare which is an essential concern of the professional early years practitioner. The content has reviewed the impact of the Plowden Report and the notion of integrated services. It has considered some theories relating to early childhood which should promote a greater understanding of how children develop and think and learn. The chapter has also focused upon key professional skills in recognizing, supporting and nurturing the individuality of the child. The professional practitioner needs to meet the challenges of diversity and reflect upon why it is important to embrace this diversity. Children's services have been characterized by professional skills and expertise in education, health and care which has been transformed into the concept of educare. In addition, the chapter has emphasized the positive aspect of this concept in approaching best practice as educare is not simply a deficit model. Continue to think about the importance of 'joined-up solutions' for 'joined-up problems' as you develop your own professional skills throughout your career in childcare.

Self-assessment questions

Question 1
What are Piaget's Stages of Development?

Question 2
How does this impact upon teaching and learning in settings?

Question 3
What impact does the Plowden Report have on education in England and Wales?

Question 4
What are the main critiques of Piaget's theories?

Question 5
Name the theorists linked with Constructivism discussed in this chapter.

Question 6
Name the theorist linked with Behaviourism discussed in this chapter.

Moving on

This chapter has introduced you to the work of some key psychologists including Piaget, Skinner and Vygotsky. Develop your understanding of this academic subject alongside the content in Chapter 6.

Further reading

Waller, T. (ed.) (2009), *An Introduction to Early Childhood*, 2nd ed. London: Sage Publications.

A good textbook that is written in clear sections, giving an overview of the terminology and concepts of Early Childhood Professional Practice.

Inclusion and Its Emergence as a Key Aspect of Best Practice

5

Chapter Outline

Learning outcomes

After reading this chapter you should be able to:

- understand the complexity in defining inclusion;
- identify how societies like the United Kingdom have evolved through reflecting on the nature of social challenges and responding accordingly by providing services for children and families;
- recognize key events in the United Kingdom such as the move away from laissez-faire to state intervention that have led to the promotion and development of an inclusive society;
- reflect on how working within early years can best support inclusive practice and diversity and in doing so demonstrate a highly valuable employability skill.

Introduction

This chapter considers how and why inclusion has become a key aspect of best practice for children's practitioners. Inclusive practice does not mean treating everyone the same way! A main theme of the chapter will be the consideration of what inclusion and inclusive practice means. At the centre of a working definition of inclusion is a belief in attempting to meet a range of diverse and at times challenging needs. This chapter explores the changing nature of society in terms of diversity as well as how society and the support services endeavour to meet the needs of the families and the individual child. Societies like the United Kingdom have evolved through reflecting on the nature of social challenges and responding accordingly by providing services for children and families. The laissez-faire notion of leaving individuals to look after themselves has been replaced by a belief in the importance of generating an inclusive society. The chapter outlines key events in the United Kingdom (such as the move away from laissez-faire to state intervention) that have led to the promotion and development of an inclusive society. The chapter explores how the changing legislation and guidance have impacted on the delivery of education and support services. It considers the influences on pedagogy and approach that have emerged in response to the needs of promoting an inclusive society within practice. The evolving nature of the language of inclusion and the impact on practice will be explored. Some of the difficulties and challenges in achieving inclusion are also outlined. The final part of the chapter explores how effective communication and working with parents and families is essential in promoting inclusive practice. This way of working within early years is a vital aspect of best practice and a highly valuable employability skill.

Reflective Activity 5.1

What do you think is the difference between *integration* and *inclusion*?

Feedback

The term inclusion is often confused with integration when in fact they are not the same! An example of integration in the United Kingdom is the attempt to give all children access to education. Inclusion is a much more encompassing term – it is about providing equality of opportunity in general. Inclusion is about providing support to overcome the barriers to equal opportunities in society.

Inclusion in society

Inclusion is an important tenet of our society – it underpins the practices and beliefs that inform and define the essence of our culture and way of life. It is the key to understanding the importance of our educare approach. It is a recognition of all children's rights and, indeed, the rights of all in wider society. Inclusion recognizes the value of the child's voice, the right to be heard and the right to have an opportunity to enjoy life. The term 'inclusion' is, however, problematic. There is no single agreed definition of the concept and that in itself presents a difficulty. How can the success of inclusive practice be measured if there is no agreement on what it exactly constitutes?

Some definitions of inclusion:

- 'Inclusive education is now concerned with establishing equity of provision for all children and rejecting the exclusion or segregation of learners for any reason whatsoever, including disability, ability, language, gender, poverty, sexuality, religion or ethnicity' (Gilson and Street (2013, p.41)).
- 'The drive towards maximum participation in and minimal exclusion from Early Years settings, from school and from society' (Nutbrown and Clough (2006, p.3)).
- Reducing barriers to learning and participation for all students, not only those with impairments or those who are categorized as 'having special educational needs' (Centre for Studies on Inclusive Education, (CSIE) on-line).
- Key words and concepts: Maximum participation, Society, provision for all, removing barriers, equity.

Although there are particular key words and concepts in these definitions, there is not an all-encompassing definition of inclusion. As such, it is important to emphasize that there is not a single agreed definition of the term 'inclusion'.

Reflective Activity 5.2

Is your own experience of education inclusive?

Feedback

Nutbrown et al. (2013) note 'cultures, communities and curricula are, by definition, exclusive. We know things by their characteristics and by the boundaries of those features; we group things, we classify' (Nutbrown et al., 2013, p.4). Therefore, how do we promote inclusion and yet maintain and celebrate diversity?

Children and childhood

Modern Western childhood is unique in that it quarantines children as a separate part of the human world. This was not always the case. Our ideas about childhood have changed over the centuries and the concept of childhood as specific strata in life emerged in the seventeenth century in Western countries. A number of philosophers influenced this understanding of childhood.

John Locke (1632–1704)

John Locke, a philosopher and influential thinker from the seventeenth century, prescribed a mixture of kindness and good sense in bringing up children. He considered that 'You must do nothing before him, which you would not have him imitate (Locke (1692, Section 71)). It must be permitted children not only to divert themselves, but to do it after their own fashion, provided it be innocently and without prejudice to their health' (Locke (1692, Section 108)). Interestingly, Locke also considered that 'the chief art is to make all that they have to do, sport and play too' (Locke (1692, Section 63)). In his *State of the Nations*, Locke envisaged a society based upon moral agreements to care for children and each other.

Rousseau (1712–1778)

Rousseau, a hugely influential philosopher from the eighteenth century, who made significant contributions to both political philosophy and moral psychology, argued that society should leave childhood to 'ripen'.

There are three key ideas that are central to Rousseau's view of children and their development.

- First, Rousseau believed in the primacy of feeling and sensation and the centrality of matters of the heart. This was radical as Rousseau lived in the era known as the 'Age of Reason', which considered science and technology as key.
- Second, Rousseau proclaimed the basic goodness of human nature and the innocence of childhood. This was against the prevailing doctrine of original sin.
- Third, Rousseau took issue with the notion that children were but imperfect adults.

The persuasiveness of Rousseau's ideas significantly influenced contemporary approaches to children and their development. We see the recognition that it is important to include as many children as possible within the fabric of the social world.

The differentiation and specialization of childhood was also influenced by the emergence of formal school education. There are continuing debates about childhood and education today in respect of formal and progressive methods of education. The formal approach to education considers that childhood is a preparation for adult roles. The progressive approach evidenced within The Plowden Report (1967) considers that children should be themselves and 'live first and foremost as children and not as future adults' (Plowden Report (1967, p.187)). Plowden recommended the establishment of EPAs (Educational Priority Areas) in response to inequality. This was a key proposal of the Plowden Report, 'one which received immediate and widespread support' (Smith (1987, p.23)).

The Education Act (1970)

The 1970 Education Act ended the long-standing practice of a small minority of children being classified as uneducable. The Act ended the understanding that children 'suffering from a disability of mind' could be classed as 'unsuitable for education at school'. For the first time in United Kingdom history, every child was entitled to an education. Discriminatory labelling, however, was still in evidence in that some children were deemed to be Educationally Sub-Normal (ESN). This resulted in them receiving their education in special schools.

The Warnock Report (1978)

It was the Warnock Report (1978) that had a significant impact on integration in schools. This was a Special Educational Needs Report of the Committee of Enquiry into the Education of Handicapped Children and Young People. The Warnock Report (1978) recognized that a child could have needs at different times – they could require support in moments of time and provided that the support was forthcoming, they could use that and move on. The Report acknowledged that children with Special Educational Needs could be provided with mainstream schooling and only a small minority would need support and facilities beyond those available. Special Schools would still be needed in these cases.

In many schools, the children were still segregated into separate units for their education. Warnock identified three main options for integration to function in schools.

- location integration – educated in a special unit in the same location;
- social integration – educated in a special unit in the same location but sharing breaks and extra-curricular activities;
- function integration – educated in a special unit in the same location but sharing some of the curriculum alongside their peers.

This model, therefore, still evidences the use of the concept 'normal' – the idea that children ought to be educated in mainstream teaching in order to have uniformity of educational experiences. This is far from the inclusive practice of today and increasingly, during the 1980s and 1990s, the notion of 'normality' was questioned. It was deemed discriminatory to label children in this way and a challenge to their human rights. The Warnock Report was not based on human rights in the sense that it considered integration good for some children but not others. What did emerge however was the emphasis placed on the importance of parental views. The report recognized the value of parental knowledge and stated that this information needed to be used in the decision-making process. This knowledge was seen as being vital to the decisions made for the child's educational future.

The Education Act 1981

The ideology of integration established in the Warnock Report (1978) is incorporated into the Education Act (1981). In addition, the Education Act also focuses on parental wishes. The Act deemed that all Local Education Authorities had to ensure that all children were educated in mainstream schools subject to some key criteria:

- the views of the child's parents have been taken into account;
- that integration was compatible with the child receiving suitable provision for their needs;
- efficient use of resources for the child and the other children being educated alongside.

The Act met with a varied response ranging from enthusiasm to resistance. It also brought with it an unprecedented level of bureaucracy. It can be argued that although some inclusion followed, this was despite the system rather than because of it. Parents had a right of appeal but again, in practice, this proved unwieldy and deeply flawed. Both the Warnock Report and the Education Act informed policy throughout the 1980s. The focus was still on 'needs' and as such this policy is still a deficit model – adjusting to needs rather than embracing the differences and recognizing the positive possibilities of inclusion.

United Nations Convention for the Rights of the Child (UNCRC) (1989)

The rights of the child are established in law and enshrined in the United Nations Convention on the Rights of the Child (UNCRC) in 1989. A child is defined as a person up to the age of eighteen. The aim is to give an equality of opportunity to all children worldwide and set out the rights of every child no matter where they lived, to grow up safe and healthy and happy. It is stated as law that governments must ensure that children do not experience discrimination and that they have a right 'to an education, to be healthy, to a childhood, to be treated fairly and to be heard' (UNICEF online). One of the clear aims of the Convention was to make children visible in the policy of the member states. This can show itself in many different ways and provides a range of opportunities from reducing infant mortality rates, to providing education for girls, to improving disability access, and more. The aims are to ensure the well-being of the child and offer the opportunity to develop to the fullest potential. To achieve this, certain goals are outlined and articulated through the Articles stated in the Convention. The United Kingdom ratified the Convention in 1991 and hence accepted the responsibility to implement and support actions that would meet these obligations. In excess of 190 countries, including the United Kingdom, signed up to the Convention and ratified the articles. Somalia, South Sudan and the United States signed the convention but it was not ratified. South Sudan and Somalia have ratified the convention fairly recently (2013) and the United States has declared its intent to do so under the Obama Administration. Huge inroads have been made, yet more needs to be done resulting in UNICEF (United Nations International Children's Emergency Fund) declaring 2014 as the 'Year for Innovation for Equality'.

Article 2 is a key statement in the consideration of inclusion in that it is clear that the children's rights apply without discrimination – the Convention applies to everyone: whatever their ethnicity, gender, religion, abilities, whatever they think or say, whatever type of family they come from.

Article 23 regarding a child's right to full social integration and independent development has been used by the United Nations Committee on the Rights of the Child as the guiding principle for inclusion.

The Convention also recognized that children are not a commodity or property of their (Table 5.1) parents nor should they be considered as helpless; rather, they are individuals with rights and with a voice. They have the same fundamental rights as adults. The Convention is the means to that voice, enshrined in international law; it aims to sustain and improve the lives of children worldwide. The countries that have signed up to the agreement have to bring their policy and practice in line with the aims and standards of the Convention. It is through this obligation that children's lives are progressed. However, it is important that not only do governments promote and adhere to the Convention but that society as a whole embraces the importance of the agreement and in doing so celebrates the rights of the child.

Table 5.1 A summary of the UN Convention on the Rights of the Child

United Nations Convention for the Rights of the Child Summary of Articles	
Article 1 (definition of the child)	Everyone under the age of 18 has all the rights in the Convention.
Article 2 (without discrimination)	The Convention applies to everyone: whatever their ethnicity, gender, religion, abilities, whatever they think or say, whatever type of family they come from.
Article 3 (best interests of the child)	The best interests of the child must be a top priority in all things that affect children.
Article 4 (protection of rights)	Governments must do all they can to make sure every child can enjoy their rights.
Article 5 (parental guidance)	Governments must respect the rights and responsibilities of parents and carers to direct and guide their child as they grow up, so that they enjoy their rights properly.
Article 6 (survival and development)	Every child has the right to life. Governments must do all they can to ensure that children survive and develop to their full potential.
Article 7 (registration, name, nationality, care)	Every child has the right to a legal name and nationality, as well as the right to know and, as far as possible, to be cared for by their parents.
Article 8 (preservation of identity)	Governments must respect and protect every child's right to an identity and prevent their name, nationality or family relationships from being changed unlawfully. If a child has been denied part of their identity illegally, governments must act quickly to protect and assist the child to re-establish their identity.
Article 9 (separation from parents)	Children must not be separated from their parents unless it is in the best interests of the child (for example, if a parent is hurting a child). Children whose parents have separated have the right to stay in contact with both parents, unless this might hurt the child.
Article 10 (family reunification)	Governments must respond quickly and sympathetically if a child or their parents apply to live together in the same country. If a child's parents live apart in different countries, the child has the right to visit both of them.
Article 11 (kidnapping and trafficking)	Governments must do everything they can to stop children being taken out of their own country illegally or being prevented from returning.
Article 12 (respect for the views of the child)	Every child has the right to say what they think in all matters affecting them and to have their views taken seriously.
Article 13 (freedom of expression)	Every child must be free to say what they think and to seek and receive all kinds of information, as long as it is within the law.
Article 14 (freedom of thought, belief and religion)	Every child has the right to think and believe what they want and also to practise their religion, as long as they are not stopping other people from enjoying their rights. Governments must respect the rights of parents to give their children information about this right.
Article 15 (freedom of association)	Every child has the right to meet with other children and to join groups and organisations, as long as this does not stop other people from enjoying their rights.
Article 16 (right to privacy)	Every child has the right to privacy. The law should protect the child's private, family and home life.

(Continued)

United Nations Convention for the Rights of the Child Summary of Articles

---

Article 17 (access to information from mass media)	Every child has the right to reliable information from the media. This should be information that children can understand. Governments must help protect children from materials that could harm them.
Article 18 (parental responsibilities; state assistance)	Both parents share responsibility for bringing up their child and should always consider what is best for the child. Governments must support parents by giving them the help they need, especially if the child's parents work.
Article 19 (protection from all forms of violence)	Governments must do all they can to ensure that children are protected from all forms of violence, abuse, neglect and bad treatment by their parents or anyone else who looks after them.
Article 20 (children deprived of a family)	If a child cannot be looked after by their family, governments must make sure that they are looked after properly by people who respect the child's religion, culture and language.
Article 21 (adoption)	If a child is adopted, the first concern must be what is best for the child. All children must be adopted and kept safe, whether they are adopted in the country where they were born or in another country.
Article 22 (refugee children)	If a child is a refugee or seeking refuge, governments must ensure that they have the same rights as any other child. Governments must help in trying to reunite child refugees with their parents. Where this is not possible, the child should be given protection.
Article 23 (children with disability)	A child with a disability has the right to live a full and decent life with dignity and independence and to play an active part in the community. Governments must do all they can to provide support to disabled children.
Article 24 (health and health services)	Every child has the right to the best possible health. Governments must provide good quality health care, clean water, nutritious food and a clean environment so that children can stay healthy. Richer countries must help poorer countries achieve this.
Article 25 (review of treatment in care)	If a child has been placed away from home (in care, hospital or prison, for example), they have the right to a regular check of their treatment and the way they are cared for.
Article 26 (social security)	Governments must provide extra money for the children of families in need.
Article 27 (adequate standard of living)	Every child has the right to a standard of living that is good enough to meet their physical, social and mental needs. Governments must help families who cannot afford to provide this.
Article 28 (right to education)	Every child has the right to an education. Primary education must be free. Secondary education must be available to every child. Discipline in schools must respect children's dignity. Richer countries must help poorer countries achieve this.
Article 29 (goals of education)	Education must develop every child's personality, talents and abilities to the full. It must encourage the child's respect for human rights, as well as respect for their parents, their own and other cultures, and the environment.
Article 30 (children of minorities)	Every child has the right to learn and use the language, customs and religion of their family, whether or not these are shared by the majority of the people in the country where they live.
Article 31 (leisure, play and culture)	Every child has the right to relax, play and take part in a wide range of cultural and artistic activities.

(Continued)

United Nations Convention for the Rights of the Child Summary of Articles

Article 32 (child labour)	Governments must protect children from work that is dangerous or might harm their health or education.
Article 33 (drug abuse)	Governments must protect children from the use of illegal drugs.
Article 34 (sexual exploitation)	Governments must protect children from sexual abuse and exploitation.
Article 35 (abduction)	Governments must ensure that children are not abducted or sold.
Article 36 (other forms of exploitation)	Governments must protect children from all other forms of bad treatment.
Article 37 (detention)	No child shall be tortured or suffer other cruel treatment or punishment. A child should be arrested only as a last resource and for the shortest possible time. Children must not be put in a prison with adults and they must be able to keep in contact with their family.
Article 38 (war and armed conflicts – see 'Optional protocols')	Governments must do everything they can to protect and care for children affected by war. Governments must not allow children under the age of 15 to take part in war or join the armed forces.
Article 39 (rehabilitation of child victims)	Children neglected, abused, exploited, tortured or who are victims of war must receive special help to help them recover their health, dignity and self-respect.
Article 40 (juvenile justice)	A child accused or guilty of breaking the law must be treated with dignity and respect. They have the right to help from a lawyer and a fair trial that takes account of their age or situation. The child's privacy must be respected at all times.
Article 41 (respect for better national standards)	If the laws of a particular country protect children better than the articles of the Convention, then those laws must stay in place.
Article 42 (knowledge of rights)	Governments must make the Convention known to children and adults.
The Convention has 54 articles in total. Articles 43–54 are about how adults and governments must work together to make sure all children get all their rights, including:	
Article 45	UNICEF can provide expert advice and assistance on children's rights.

Source: 'A summary of the UN Convention on the Rights of the Child' Leaflet, https://www.unicef.org.United Kingdom/ Documents/Publication-pdfs/betterlifeleaflet2012_press.pdf

1993 Education Act

The Audit Commission reviewed the implementation processes of the 1981 Education Act in 1992. The Commission concluded that inspection procedures were weak and reviews, as a result, flawed. The subsequent 1993 Education Act attempted to improve on these areas and in particular gave a stronger voice to parents. While the three conditions linked to the 1981 Act remained, an essential element of this new Act, the additional phrase 'unless it is incompatible with the wishes of the parents' was added reflecting the importance now given to the parental voice.

1994 The Salamanca Statement

This was an incredibly influential international document and the catalyst for much of the educational policy aimed at delivering inclusive practice in schools in the United Kingdom. It was delivered at the World Conference on Special Needs and was a reaffirmation by ninety-two governments and twenty-five organizations of their commitment to 'Education for All'. The Conference adopted The Salamanca Statement on Principles, Policy and Practice in Special Needs Education and, a second document, A Framework for Action. Since this was linked through the UN, the statements carried with them a human rights issue – the concept that society was moving towards inclusivity rather than just education, yet schools were seen as the key means in delivering and supporting this inclusive society.

Statement 2 of the Salamanca Agreement outlined the commitment:

> • every child has a fundamental right to education, and must be given the opportunity to achieve and maintain an acceptable level of learning;
> • every child has unique characteristics, interests, abilities and learning needs;
> • education systems should be designed and educational programmes implemented to take into account the wide diversity of these characteristics and needs;
> • those with special educational needs must have access to regular schools which should accommodate them within a child-centred pedagogy capable of meeting these needs;
> • regular schools with this inclusive orientation are the most effective means of combating discriminatory attitudes, creating welcoming communities, building an inclusive society and achieving education for all; moreover, they provide an effective education to the majority of children and improve the efficiency and ultimately the cost-effectiveness of the entire education system.
>
> (Article 2, Salamanca Statement, (1994))

The Statement called on governments to:

> • give the highest policy and budgetary priority to improve their education systems to enable them to include all children regardless of individual differences or difficulties;
> • adopt as a matter of law or policy the principle of inclusive education, enrolling all children in regular schools, unless there are compelling reasons for doing otherwise'.
>
> (Article 3, Salamanca Statement, (1994))

It should also be noted that the final statement in Article 2 recognizes that the inclusive policy should achieve effective education for the majority of children – an acceptance that actually it is not for all? The implications are that the needs of most children are best served through this policy but that would still leave a minority, by definition, that inclusive schooling would not best serve.

In addition, the Statement also specifically recognizes the role of the parents in their child's education and that their involvement in the decision-making process should be encouraged and facilitated. What is also interesting is that the demands for change were rooted in society as well through pressure groups, parents and other supporters. The Salamanca Agreement gave children a means of having a voice.

Green Paper: Excellence For All Children (1997)

In this document, David Blunkett acknowledges that

> while recognising the paramount importance of meeting the needs of individual children, and the necessity of specialist provision for some, we shall promote the inclusion of children with SEN within mainstream schooling wherever possible. We shall remove barriers which get in the way of meeting the needs of all children and re-define the role of special schools to develop a network of specialist support.
> (DfES, 1997, p.5) [Note the use of the word 'inclusion'.]

Special Educational Needs and the Disability Act – 2001 (SENDA)

The Special Educational Needs and the Disability Act (2001) Part 1 strengthened the right to inclusive education and, in addition, called for a radical and inclusive approach to school design. The Act repealed some of the provisos in the 1996 Education Act which strengthened the right to mainstream schooling. However, two conditions remained:

A disabled child can only go to a mainstream school on condition that:

- it is compatible with the parent's wishes, and
- there is an efficient education of other children.

Again, note the importance of parents in the decision-making process.

A revised code of practice on SEN came into effect in 2002 based on the SENDA principles and incorporating the new SEN regulations which made inclusion more of a legal requirement.

The Education Act (1996)

This demonstrated another shift in UK society's approach to education in terms of inclusive policy. Local authorities had to place all children in mainstream schools (unless this was incompatible with efficient use of resources or against the wishes of the parents). This represents a succinct yet highly important difference in approach.

Evaluating Educational Inclusion (2000) (OFSTED)

This document presented a view of inclusion that was far broader than educational needs. It focused on *equal opportunities for all pupils, whatever their age, gender, ethnicity, attainment and background.*

'Special educational needs: a new look' – (2005) – a pamphlet – Warnock revisited

In 2005, Baroness Warnock revisited the argument on inclusion when she published a pamphlet, 'Special educational needs: a new look'. This pamphlet reconsidered both inclusion and statementing and suggested that the number of statements had been far in excess of what had been envisaged. Warnock advocated that the approach to inclusion be reviewed with some urgency in order to meet the diverse needs of the child. Bullying of children in mainstream schools was regarded as being almost inevitable and inclusion was recommended as being a 'feeling of belonging' that is necessary for well-being and successful learning. Warnock's intervention at this stage was, however, criticized in that some of the factual data seemed to be dated. This undermined the credibility of her critique. What was apparent, however, was that the basic problems that were alluded to (a bloated bureaucracy and a constant battle for resources) had some foundation.

Every Child Matters: Change For Children (2004)

The main focus areas were early intervention, a shared sense of responsibility, information sharing and integrated front line services.

Framework for the Early Years Foundation Stage (EYFS) 2008

The stated purpose and aim of the framework was to help all children achieve the five principles of Every Child Matters. This included provision 'for equality of opportunity and anti-discriminatory practice and ensuring that every child is included and not disadvantaged because of ethnicity, culture or religion, home language, family background, learning difficulties or disabilities, gender or ability' (EYFS, 2003, p.7).

Statutory framework for the Early Years Foundation Stage (EYFS) 2012

The Early Years Framework was revised in 2012 following recommendations from the Tickell Review in 2011. The reforms were expected to reduce the paperwork and bureaucracy but also had other intentions including the aim to strengthen partnerships between parents and professionals. The four guiding principles recognized the individual child as a unique child and that the child would flourish through positive relationships and by being provided with an enabling environment. There was a recognition that children learnt in different ways and at different rates. It is thus possible to see that society and education have changed through the generations in moving to educate all children, then to integrate all children and finally to the inclusive practice envisaged today. An inclusive society is evidenced by an inclusive educational policy. The ideal of 'including all children' however, remains a challenge. Early years remains at the forefront of inclusive education. However, while the government is making these clear statements regarding inclusion the practitioner needs to actually action inclusive practice.

Inclusion and diversity

Increasingly, inclusion is recognized as being more than 'Special Educational Needs'. The groups who are considered within the concept of inclusion can be defined by their culture and physical abilities but it would be a mistake to only consider diversity as race and culture. In fact, a limitation of the interpretation of diversity is that it can promote a tendency to reinforce a stereotype. This must be avoided! Inclusion is about all children.

The understanding of inclusion in practice has moved from a medical model to a social model. This has clearly been reflected in the changes to legislation and the curriculum. The medical model is a more rigid interpretation of ability. Criteria appear to be fixed and rigid. In contrast, the social model appears to be more flexible. Identity is regarded as being socially constructed. Differences are celebrated and embraced. However, while the medical model does not require society to change, the social model is dependent on society being prepared and willing to change. This is reflected in the both the international and UK agreements reached and legislation implemented, particularly in the last two decades. That is not to say that inclusion is complete – it is an ongoing evolutionary ideal that societies aspire towards. The concept of the medical and social models still retains the focus of inclusion on disability. However, inclusion is also about enabling diversity. The notion of inclusion in education is based on the principle of enabling diversity.

The Ofsted Report 'Evaluating Educational Inclusion (OFSTED 2000)' embraces a wider view of inclusion.

> Educational inclusion is more than a concern about any one group of pupils such as those pupils who have been or are likely to be excluded from school. Its scope is broad. It is about equal opportunities for all pupils, whatever their age, gender, ethnicity, attainment and background. It pays particular attention to the provision made for and the achievement of different groups of pupils within a school. Throughout this guidance, whenever we use the term different groups it could apply to any or all of the following:
>
> • girls and boys;
> • minority ethnic and faith groups, Travellers, asylum seekers and refugees;

- pupils who need support to learn English as an additional language (EAL);
- pupils with special educational needs;
- gifted and talented pupils;
- children 'looked after' by the local authority;
- other children, such as sick children; young carers; those children from families under stress; pregnant school girls and teenage mothers; and
- any pupils who are at risk of disaffection and exclusion.

(Ofsted, 2000, p.4)

In 2000, a toolkit of materials, 'Index for Inclusion: developing learning and participation in schools', was developed and placed in every school and Local Education Authority. The intention was to help and support the development of inclusive practice in schools. The aim was to enable all pupils to participate as fully as possible by removing the barriers to their participation and learning. The toolkit was published by the Centre for Studies on Inclusive Education (CSIE), who considered the process as being about 'building supportive communities and fostering high achievement for all staff and students' (Booth and Ainscow (2000)). The materials were intended to enable settings to 'adopt a self-review approach to analyse their cultures policies and practices and to identify the barriers to learning and participation' (Booth and Ainscow (2000)). This approach to inclusion adopts a social model perspective and yet the understanding of the term 'inclusion' remains fluid. A list of concepts appears in the document, giving a range of inclusive ideals including valuing all students and staff, increasing participation in the curriculum and recognizing that inclusion in education is linked to inclusion in society.

What factors contribute to children being different from each other?

There are many factors that can contribute to this and a truly inclusive society and education will respond to these factors. Essentially there are two main components – extrinsic and intrinsic factors. An indication of these is given below:

Extrinsic factors (conditioning or determining factors)

- Nationality.
- Geography – where the child lives.

- Economic impact – e.g. poverty, household income.
- Culture and Ethnicity.
- Social – relating to class, family background, etc.

Intrinsic factors (individual or specific factors)

- Physically – genetic factors, disability issues, etc.
- Health – the impact of health issues, restriction of access, interventions needed, etc.
- Social and emotional well-being.
- Cognition issues – based on ability, identified special needs, etc.

Reflective Activity 5.3

When did you first realize you were 'different'?
Was this a positive or negative experience?

The employability agenda

While the emergence of the inclusive agenda can be tracked through the changes in legislation, guidance and policy at both national and international levels, there are barriers to its effective delivery. Devarakonda (2013) contends that policy can change in the journey from the policy maker to the grass roots. 'The policy cascading from global to national, and then to regional to local and then to the early childhood setting will lead to the policy being diluted and perhaps misinterpreted' (Devarakonda (2013, p.4)). In addition, a lack of awareness of the social issues around inclusive practice will have a profound effect on children and families. This could be reduced by the encouragement of a reflective practitioner: one who reflects on practice and constantly reappraises intent and delivery and seeks improvement. It should also be acknowledged that practitioners are part of society and therefore have the challenge, when trying to effect change, of stepping outside their own possible prejudices and perceptions. 'For example, assumptions about certain groups in society will create barriers to the provision of equal opportunities for children in these groups' (Tedam, 2009, p.123).

Parents as partners

The UN Convention highlights and defends the family's role in the lives of children. Throughout the growing understanding of the value of inclusive practice both in society and in education, the involvement and voice of both child and parents has been central. This was embraced in the Early Years Foundation Document where the Partnership with Parents was recognized as a key to effective progress. 'Parents are children's first and most enduring educators. When parents and practitioners work together in early years settings, the results have a positive impact on children's development and learning' (EYFS, 2003, p.2). The document also states that the diversity of the individual children and communities should be respected and that the no family or child should be discriminated against.

In the Statutory Framework for the Early Years Foundation Stage document, the need to work in partnership with parents is again clearly stated. The concept of planning for the needs of the individual child is cited and specific reference is made to inclusive practice in the stated aim involving equality of opportunity.

The EYFS seeks to provide:

- quality and consistency in all early years settings so that every child makes good progress and no child gets left behind;
- a secure foundation through learning and development opportunities which are planned around the needs and interests of each individual child and are assessed and reviewed regularly;

• partnership working between practitioners and with parents and/or carers;
• equality of opportunity and anti-discriminatory practice, ensuring that every child is included and supported.

(EYFS, 2003, p.2)

The Framework became mandatory in September 2012. One of the overarching principles is that every child is unique. Fitzgerald states that all parties need to have a shared understanding of what partnership means to them in order to work effectively together and that 'for partnerships to be maintained, it is vital that there are effective strategies in place to facilitate two-directional communication and support. This is especially critical in early years environments, as for many families it is likely to be their first contact with education and care settings' Fitzgerald (2004, p.21).

Reflective Activity 5.5

What do you think a partnership is?
Do partners in personal relationships have the same criteria and functions as those in a business or in public service?
What are the key features of an effective partnership?

Feedback

In effective partnership everyone needs to understand:

• How they fit into the partnership.
• What they bring to the agenda.
• What their motivation is.
• What they feel about it (their emotional link).
• What information/knowledge they have.
• How they will work together.

This can only be done if all parties are 'talking' to each other.

The practitioner can try to ensure that the conversations are two-directional and also those conversations can be formal or informal. The parent needs to feel at ease when discussing their child and what they anticipate to be the child's requirements. They also need to be confident that their views are being listened to and their points discussed. This does not mean everything the parent advocates is possible or even best practice, but the parent should feel that the views have been considered and should be afforded the courtesy of discussion.

Principles of partnership

It is important when working with parents to focus on the family and the child and to treat them with respect. It is therefore useful to work within some guiding principles:

- Respect for children as diverse individuals.
- Respect for the different ways different parents have of loving and caring for children.
- Willingness to relate to children and parents in diverse ways.
- Respect for parents' decisions about their own lives.
- Commitment to communicate on a regular basis in a courteous manner.
- Commitment to listen to parents' views about the early years setting and act on their concerns.
- Acknowledge that there are the different views about childhood, child-rearing practices and learning goals, roles of parents and roles of practitioners.
- Clear communication about ways in which each can help the other in the partnership.
- Clear procedures to support parents to become involved.
- Clear communication channels for parents and practitioners. Be prepared to explain to parents about the records, the procedures and actions that are undertaken.

Underpinning some of these guiding principles is the important acknowledgement that the practitioner should not make moral judgements about different approaches to childcare. It is important to recognize that there are different cultural values. A range of values is present within any society and it is important to consider these differences with an open mind. The partnership between practitioners, other agencies and parents may not always function equally because of the various differences between individuals.

Inclusive settings

'Difference is of interest to children, and the recognition of difference as positive rather than negative is an important aim for early childhood professionals' (Nutbrown et al. (2013, p.13)). An inclusive setting will focus on supporting the positive aspects of difference and try to remove the barriers that prevent the child from progressing or accessing some of the opportunities. The social benefits of an inclusive setting are also important. Where a setting can demonstrate the acceptance of diversity, the children's experience of this acceptance is likely to become manifest in its dealings with wider society. The acceptance of others in friendship and within the boundaries of the setting, whether it be gender, cultural differences, class, income, ethnicity etc. becomes the norm. The children's experiences and expectations are broadened and become more accepting. 'It is equally important to acknowledge that inclusion also benefits children without disabilities. When placed in inclusive settings, young children are more accepting of children with disabilities' (Vakil et al. (2003, p.187)).

Inclusive play – the role of the practitioner

The concept of 'inclusive play' is as elusive as the term inclusion in that there is no agreed definition. This is in itself, therefore, a challenge to the practitioner.

However, guidance with the EYFS regards an enabling environment as one of the overarching principles.

> children learn and develop well in enabling environments, in which their experiences respond to their individual needs and there is a strong partnership between practitioners and parents and/or carers. (DfE (2012, p.3))

It is important for the practitioner to provide an enabling environment in order to support inclusive play. The environment can be changed to meet diverse needs and promote the opportunities for the child to investigate, experiment, role play, socially interact with their peers and much more. It can explore a variety of sensory approaches which, again, can accommodate diversity. 'A rich play environment creates opportunities for children to follow a number of paths through their explorations and discoveries to open-ended destinations' (Casey (2010, p.21)). The richer the environment, the greater the possibility that the child can learn and develop within the space, and an acceptance by peers when in play can raise self-esteem. When children are at play within the environment, the practitioner can use the opportunities to observe the child, to be aware of progress and to intervene as required. The practitioner should also promote the use of the space so that it is used effectively by responding to the individual child's needs. Therefore, providing this environment is a key part of the role of the practitioner. The idea that a child has a voice and can participate so effectively in their own learning and development is testament to the need to provide the opportunities and enable the inclusive play.

A key principle is for practitioners to have an understanding of children's perceptions of them. The differences need to be embraced and not ignored. The emphasis is not so much on changing the child but providing an enabling environment that will allow the child to flourish and develop. This does not negate the need for high aspirations for all children but does preclude the drive to homogenize children. Practitioners are not attempting to make all the children the same! At times, this is a difficult and challenging agenda as their practice in the settings should mirror society but often is, in fact, challenging society's preconceptions and leading change. The responsibility of good inclusive practice, therefore, is more than just a commitment to the child but, indeed, a commitment to a belief within society itself. Society, in turn, needs to be committed to the concept of inclusive practice. To enable this symbiotic relationship involves social, moral and ethical choices. It is a question of upholding and maintaining children's rights – their right for respect and to be treated with equal value and society needs to support this philosophy. Education needs to be adapted to the child and not the opposite. The focus for the practitioner is on the possibilities rather than the limitations.

Inclusion – an ongoing challenge

Inclusion remains an ongoing challenge for the practitioner at a practical level. There is within practice a difficulty in meeting all the agendas – to raise attainment and meet specific targets within a pre-determined time frame, to embrace the differences but still provide opportunities, to support a child when sometimes that stops at the setting boundaries. All these are challenges for the practitioner. This is also complicated by the government's standards agenda – the need to meet targets and the accountability for attainment that does not seem to be related to the challenges associated with the school's catchment area or the pupil's diversity of needs. In addition, an increasingly restricted curriculum, again related to levels and targets, presents pedagogical challenges for the practitioner in trying to present a diverse, challenging yet fulfilling curriculum.

It is also important to note that the lack of a clear, agreed definition for inclusion makes it difficult to evaluate. To know if inclusion is working requires consensus about both the terminology and the criteria upon which to judge its success. While the key to success is often linked to early identification and intervention – how do we know?

The fact that inclusion is at least on the agenda, that it is debated, that society does support the principles of a child's rights is clearly a positive move in the right direction. Inclusion remains an ongoing process – a constant striving for the ideal.

Self-assessment questions

Complete the following sentences.

Question 1
Integration is.............................

Question 2
Inclusion is.............................

Question 3
What were the three key ideas central to Rousseau's view of children and their development?

Question 4
What was the date of the Warnock Report?

Question 5
The Warnock Report considered integration in education. Another important issue was the recognition of ....

Question 6
What were the two main pieces of international legislation that strengthened the case for inclusion in the United Kingdom?

Question 7
What were two of the important commitments from the Salamanca Statement relating to education and children?

Question 8

The Salamanca Statement also recognized the importance of whose role in the education of the child?

Question 9

In the Special Educational Needs and Disability Act (2001) (SENDA), which two conditions remained as a proviso for children to be entitled to a mainstream education?

Moving on

This chapter has explored the concept of inclusion and diversity. Inclusion is evidenced within society and links to multi-agency working. This philosophy informs planning and management in settings as it entails removing barriers for all children to enable them to have an opportunity to reach their full potential. Practitioners need to strive for fairness and appreciate that not all children can start from the same position. It is important to provide an enabling environment that gives opportunity for all children to flourish. The chapter also focuses on the involvement of others outside the setting including parents and other agencies. Continue to think about how to provide an enabling environment, how to encourage children to develop and learn to the best of their ability and how to remove the barriers that could prevent children from reaching their full potential. This involves developing your own skills as well as giving children the chance to flourish.

Further reading

Nutbrown, C., Cough, P. and Atherton, F. (2013), *Inclusion in the Early Years*, 2nd ed. London: Sage.

A good textbook that is written considering the challenges and opportunities of inclusive practice and how this has impacted on the society and delivery within early years.

6

The Rising Importance of Holistic Practice in Early Childhood Studies

Chapter Outline

Learning outcomes

After reading this chapter you should be able to:

- identify how psychology helps us to develop holistic practice when we are working with children and families;
- analyse the benefits of holistic practice when we are working with children and families;
- critically appraise the contribution made by psychology to holistic practice when we are working with children and families.

This chapter develops your knowledge and understanding of selected psychological theories accounting for children's growth and development. The material in the chapter explores the idea that an increased awareness of applied psychology enables us to apply holistic practice when we are working with children and families. 'Holistic practice' refers to the combination of ideas and professionals who come together in a complementary way to provide services for children and families. The chapter content embellishes some of the psychological theory that has been introduced already in the book (for example in Chapters 3 and 4). In this chapter we want you to think about how the various ideas in psychology can be blended together to form a holistic practice.

Introduction

A key concept within children's services is the 'multidisciplinary team'. This term refers to the variety of professionals from health, education and care who attempt to meet the physical, intellectual, emotional and social needs of children and families. The chapter explores the merits of the holistic philosophy upon which this approach to working with children and families is based. As opposed to applying one way of working with children and families, the holistic approach combines talents and skills in order to meet needs as fully as possible. The chapter identifies the evolution of this concept within children's services. Awareness of this holistic way of working is of benefit to practitioners. It enables them to be part of the current *zeitgeist* of children's services and thus enhances best practice and employability. Throughout the chapter, there are formative activities that reinforce learning in relation to the main psychological paradigms (or models) that are of relevance for developing holistic practice for early years practitioners.

Defining the discipline of psychology

Reflective Activity 6.1

From your previous reading, what is your understanding of the word psychology?

Feedback

Psychology is an academic subject that is associated with the study of a vast range of human and animal behaviour. Psychologists are not mind readers and they do not necessarily have access to our thoughts. They do not work solely with people who are mentally ill or emotionally disturbed. These are common delusions and misinterpretations of the discipline.

'Psychology' is not as easy to define as it might initially appear. It is more than just a word. To a layperson, an immediate reaction may be to associate psychology with 'reading peoples' minds' or 'analysing aspects of human behaviour'. A dictionary definition of psychology may give a precise explanation but this precision can disguise the complexity of the subject. An example of a dictionary definition is that psychology can be understood as being 'the scientific study of all forms of human and animal behaviour' (online dictionary).

Psychology is relevant for early years practitioners because it gives explanations for children's growth and development. It is also the discipline that gives us holistic practice when we are working with children and families. This allows us to develop our understanding of how holistic practice can be applied to working with children and families. Studying psychology enables you to increase your knowledge of key factors influencing the development of children and families. Practitioners working with children and families may be able to increase their awareness of what influences the developing child and family life by considering the theories that have been generated by the discipline of psychology.

The academic discipline of psychology

The word 'psychology' comes from two Greek words 'psyche', meaning mind, and 'logos', meaning study: so, a literal translation of the discipline is 'the study of the mind'. Psychology literally translates as the study of the mind. Malim and Birch (1998, p.3) note that the academic study of psychology began in 1879 when Wilhelm Wundt opened the first psychology laboratory at the University of Leipzig in Germany. Wundt was interested in 'introspection', or the observation and analysis of conscious mental processes. It was the emphasis placed upon measurement and control of thinking processes that marked the separation of psychology from its parent discipline, philosophy.

The importance of behaviourism for holistic practice

Malim and Birch (1998, p.8) argue that by 1920, the usefulness of 'introspection' was questioned. John B. Watson was one of a number of theorists who argued that it was wrong to focus upon introspection because this approach to studying psychology cannot be measured. This makes introspection 'unscientific'. Consequently, Watson dedicated himself to the study of what has become known as 'behaviourism' –human behaviour that is measurable and observable. Behaviourism remained the dominant force in psychology over the next thirty years, especially in the United States. An emphasis was placed upon identifying the external factors that produce changes in behaviour, learning or conditioning using a stimuli–response model. This awareness of behaviourism is a key ingredient in holistic practice.

Competing but complementary perspectives

If we are to develop an awareness of holistic practice when we are working with children and families, we need to recognize how competing theories and ideas combine together to produce an understanding of 'best practice'. As with many philosophical and sociological perspectives, psychology is characterized by competing paradigms or models of thought, with theorists becoming grouped together according to the perspective they prefer. Malim and Birch (1998, p.9) argue that an interesting reaction to behaviourism came in the form of the Gestalt school of psychology emerging in Austria and Germany in the 1920s. This movement in psychology was popularized by psychologists such as Wolfgang Kohler (1927). This branch of psychology takes a holistic approach considering that the person is in totality greater and more complex than his or her individual characteristics. This in turn complicates a focus upon the external factors producing thoughts and behaviour.

Psychodynamic psychology

A critique of behaviourism developed through the twentieth century as a result of the legacy of Sigmund Freud. Freud is perhaps the most famous psychologist of all. Malim and Birch (1998, p.9) argue that Freud sees the human mind as a combination of 'conscious' (or 'awake') and 'unconscious' (or 'not awake') thoughts. If we accept that this is the case, Freud's theory can be used to challenge the ideas of behaviourism because the notion of 'conscious' and 'unconscious' thoughts reveals that human thought and behaviour is more complex than the behaviourist notion that 'external stimuli' produce 'thoughts' and 'behaviour'. A second component (psychodynamic theory) is in turn added to our understanding of holistic practice.

Cognitive psychology

Alongside psychodynamic theory, there emerged a further significant theory that places an emphasis upon thinking processes or cognition. Attention is given to the ways in which we attain, retain and regain information. Within cognitive psychology, an emphasis is placed on identifying what happens within the mind after a stimulus has been received. The mind is viewed as an information processor, almost akin to a computer. Malim and Birch (1998, p.25) explain this psychological theory by arguing that 'human beings are seen as information processors who absorb information from the outside world, code and interpret it, store and retrieve it'. In a literal revolution of thought, thinking has come back full circle and the initial criticism of 'introspection' (or the observation and analysis of conscious mental processes) is asserted within this psychological model. This third theory of the human mind adds a further layer to our understanding of holistic professional practice.

Biological psychology

Biological psychologists are interested in how biological factors inform thinking processes. The scientific advances of the 1990s and beyond in relation to identifying the genetic and hormonal composition of the human mind have generated enormous interest in the idea that thoughts and behaviour are determined by our biology. This may be considered to be a reductionist argument because it reduces complex thoughts and behaviour to a few variables such as hormones chromosomes and genes. The ideas within biological psychology may prove to be yet another passing model contributing to the ongoing dialogue about the discipline of psychology that in turn will be criticized and revised. If we are to embrace holistic practice, it is important to consider the ideas within each of the key psychological models. It is regarded as being 'best practice' if these ideas are then used to inform our professional practice when we are working with children and families in education, health and social care.

From this initial discussion about what is meant by the word 'psychology', we can ask a further question in relation to the nature of the human mind: 'Is the human mind the same as the human brain?'

Reflective Activity 6.2

Do you think that the mind is the same as the brain? Provide a rationale as to why the mind may be regarded as being the same as the brain. Why might an argument be developed that essentially argues that the mind is different to the brain?

Feedback

One answer to this question is that there is no definite answer. Philosophers have speculated for thousands of years about what has come to be known as 'the mind-brain problem' –whether you focus upon the mind or the brain depends upon your fundamental understanding of how psychology should be studied. The psychological perspectives of behaviourism, humanism, psychodynamic and cognitive theories emphasize the importance of studying the mind. This is because each of these psychological theories has a clear understanding of the mind. In contrast, biological perspectives are more likely to place an emphasis upon the genes, chromosomes and hormones influencing the brain, which in turn make us have our thoughts.

We can now look at studying the psychological theories that contribute to our understanding of holistic practice. This is a way of adding detail to our introductory explanations of psychology. It is also a means of identifying how we can use psychology to become aware of holism and best practice. Although previous chapters in the book have applied psychological theory to learning and teaching in early years, this next section gives a more detailed reflection on key ideas within the psychological schools of thought.

The schools of psychology

In the following table, there is a summary of five major schools of psychology together with a brief description of their key features.

These schools of thought are especially useful to practitioners working with children and families because of the influence they have had in shaping the nature of professional work with children and families. The practical application of this academic discipline appears to relate to much of the work that is undertaken with children and families. If you are working with children and families, you will need to apply psychology through 'modelling' best practice and meeting the needs of children and families through applying holistic practice. Knowledge and understanding of the competing perspectives in psychology can help you to achieve this 'best practice'. The origins of the schools of thought go back to some of the earliest philosophical ideas that have influenced Western thought. The proposition that there are forces beyond the individual that shape social reality goes back to the ideas of the Greek philosopher

Plato. This idea is central to behaviourism, so the perspective has its intellectual origins in this classical thought. The notion that individuals interpret their social world as opposed to being ultimately shaped by this world goes back to the ideas of Aristotle (Audi, 1995). This philosophy is of central importance to humanism. In other words, the origins of the perspective's dominant idea can be traced back to these early times. As each of these ideas in psychology contributes to our understanding of holistic practice when we are working with children and families, a summary of each of the key perspectives in the Table 6.1 follows. A definition of each of the key perspectives is given, key figures influencing the perspectives are identified and the central terms within each perspective are then explained. The definitions that are given may help you to understand the other chapters in the book that are based on psychological theories, learning and teaching.

Behaviourism

Behaviourists explore they ways that external factors produce thoughts within the human mind. A key behaviourist idea is that every individual enters the world as a 'clean slate'. The surrounding environment is regarded as being the 'chalk' etching its marks upon the 'slate' of the mind. The individual is regarded as entering the world without a fixed identity. Social factors are responsible for

Table 6.1 Schools of psychology

School	Key features
Behaviourism	Human behaviour is regarded as being shaped by external or 'environmental' forces. This behaviour is regarded as being a collection of learned responses to external stimuli. The key learning process is known as 'conditioning'.
Humanism	The individual is regarded as being unique, rational and self-determining and present experience is considered to be as important as past experience.
Psychodynamic theory	The mind is visualised as being a combination of conscious thoughts and the workings of the unconscious mind. The unconscious mind expresses itself through dreams and behaviour we are not consciously aware of (for example through fantasies).
Cognitive theory	This psychological perspective explores what happens after a stimulus but before a response. The human mind is likened to a computer. People are regarded as being like information processors who select, code, store and retrieve information when needed.
Biological theory	Behaviour is considered to be determined by genetic, physiological and neurobiological factors and processes.

making the individual whosoever s/he becomes. The Jesuit notion of 'give me the boy and I'll show you the man' equates to this idea. This suggests that we become who we are as a result of factors beyond and outside individuals.

A number of psychologists have become associated with the behaviourist school of thought. Burrhus Skinner, Edward Thorndike, John Watson and Ivan Pavlov are all synonymous with behaviourist psychology. Each of these psychologists explore how external factors produce thoughts and behaviour.

The terms 'classical conditioning' and 'operant conditioning' are particularly important within behaviourism. Classical conditioning is associated with the work of Ivan Pavlov. Classical conditioning examines how biological responses are influenced by external factors. There is what is phrased as a 'conditioned response' as forms of behaviour occur in association with a particular stimulus. Operant conditioning is associated with the work of Burrhus Skinner. The term refers to the link that exists between positively affirming behaviour that is associated with a desirable response. To give a simple example, if a child responds favourably to a parental instruction, the child is usually praised. This reinforcement of learning through praise is therefore a type of operant conditioning. In the following case study, there is the exemplification of when children may experience classical and operant conditioning.

Case study

Joanne is four years old and she has just started school. She has been in the school for one month and she has already learned many of the school rules. She has noticed that when the school bell rings at 9 am, she has to line up with all the other children and stand still with her arms by her side looking out for her class teacher Miss Killoury. At first, a number of the infants did not know what to do when the bell rang at the start of the school day. The sight of all the other children moving into line upset some of the children as they felt afraid and anxious because they did not know what they were supposed to do. This association of the bell ringing and anxiety has gradually made the infants copy what the other older children do. Today when the bell rang at 9 am nearly all of the infants copied the other older children so that they would not stand out and feel anxious. They got into line standing with their arms by their sides looking out for Miss Killoury. They moved a little bit more than the other older children but their response to the bell ringing at 9 am has become conditioned into acceptable behaviour. On Friday, Joanne received a 'star badge' for her good work. She felt very pleased as she had to go onto the stage at assembly and receive her gold badge. Joanne remembered her parents' words that in school she should always try her hardest.

Reflective Activity 6.3

What would interest behaviourist psychologists about Joanne?

Feedback

Behaviourist psychology is associated with classical and operant conditioning. A simple understanding of these two types of conditioning is that whereas classical conditioning is interested in how biological reactions are influenced by external factors, operant conditioning is concerned with how choices are influenced by external factors. The case study is relevant to both types of conditioning. The 'fear' and 'anxiety' produced by the external environment (or school) is a physical response that is generated by an external factor. The 'learned response' by Joanne to 'try her hardest' is an example of operant conditioning. Becoming aware of behaviourist theory and its implications for early years is one of the key ingredients of holistic professional practice.

Humanism

Humanism does acknowledge the importance of environmental factors on the mind, but it places an emphasis upon the individual interpretation of external factors. As opposed to emphasizing the importance of external variables, attention is given to the importance of individuals interpreting social reality. Humanism links to the philosophy of Immanuel Kant and his 'Copernican revolution' of thought (Audi, 1995, p.400). As opposed to asking about the reality of the universe, Kant changes the focus of the argument to ask about how individuals understand the social world. Humanism asks a similar question. As opposed to focusing upon how external variables produce thoughts, the humanist emphasis is on how individuals make sense of external variables.

Humanism has become associated with the work of Carl Rogers and Abraham Maslow. Maslow proposes that all humans have a 'hierarchy of needs' and that individual thoughts are influenced by the extent to which these physiological and intellectual needs are being met. Carl Rogers has had a particularly important influence on humanism and it may be claimed that Rogers is the psychologist who is most associated with humanism. His work is also influential in what is considered to be 'effective practice' when we are working with children and families. One of the most important Rogerian ideas to have influenced social care is the proposal that anxiety is a product of what has become termed as a 'would/should dilemma'. The would/should dilemma proposes that although an individual wants to do something, they are unable to achieve this wish. According to Rogers, this in turn generates tension within the individual that then produces anxiety.

In applying therapy to resolve the would/should dilemma, Rogers recommends that the therapist must have a 'congruent' or genuine interest in the person. Empathy is a central concept to the Rogerian model of client-centred therapy. The ideal aim is to lead the person being counselled to their 'inner beautiful self' so that the individual's would/should dilemma can be overcome.

Reflective Activity 6.4

Think about your own personal development. To what extent do you think that your personality has been formed as a result of external environmental factors? To what extent do you think that your personality is a product of your unique personality?

Feedback

Most people would probably agree that their personality is a combination of external environmental variables alongside their own unique personal traits. In other words, the person is a product of factors that are both outside and inside the individual. It is interesting, however, to consider why and when the emphasis placed upon the individual and the environment varies. In this country, particular social, economic and religious variables have influenced the extent to which one's surroundings or one's personality are held accountable for personality development. In the UK there are many communities that emphasize self-responsibility. If one claims that the environment is responsible for personal development, this may be regarded as an attempt to disown one's accountability for individual life circumstances. Some of the popular movements of the 1960s and 1970s may have changed this perception but the prevailing thought in the UK today appears to be that individual characteristics are especially important in determining one's personality. This may lessen the importance of the behaviourist perspective and make humanism a more influential explanation of individual circumstances. The best advice (if we are to apply the ideas of holistic practice) is to make sure that both of the theories are combined and applied with other psychological perspectives. This will help us to ensure that our work with children and families is characterized by being based on a combination of theories and practical interventions.

Psychodynamic theory

Psychodynamic psychology is associated with the ideas of one of the most famous psychologists, Sigmund Freud. Freud's theory is based on the idea that our thoughts are a product of the workings of the conscious and the unconscious mind (Gross, 2010, p.969). We have conscious thoughts that we are aware of and unconscious thoughts that appear in our mind in the form of dreams. Moreover, what happens in our conscious mind in turn influences what thoughts filter through to our unconscious mind.

Freud considers that there are three especially important components to every individual (Gross, 2010, p.591). There is the 'id', or biological physiology of maleness and femaleness. There is the 'ego', or social self, to regulate our biological 'id'. There is also the 'superego' existing beyond the individual that generates a common understanding of our social identity.

Freud claims that all individuals go through a number of stages of development. From 0 to 1, a child is considered to be in an oral stage of development. The child is preoccupied with its mouth. The anal stage of development is from one to two when the infant becomes aware of its capacity to excrete and urinate. The next developmental stage is the phallic stage of development when boys and girls become increasingly aware of biological maleness and femaleness. Freud claims that this stage of development occurs between the ages of three and six. This stage of development is associated with the developing relationship between a boy and his mother and a girl and her father. After the phallic stage of development, there is what Freud terms as a latent phase of development. This occurs between the ages of six and twelve as the individual becomes more concerned with their social identity as they become increasingly aware of their ego state. The theory states that the final stage of development is the genital stage, from the age of twelve onwards when Freud proposes that males and females become increasingly aware of their adult reproductive capabilities.

Freud's theory introduces the idea that human beings hold the potential for fixated behaviour. Freud proposes that an individual is capable of becoming negatively confined to a particular stage (or stages) of development. As an example, if an infant experienced the trauma of losing its mother at the age of one, there is the possibility of this individual developing what Freud terms an 'oral fixation'. This fixated behaviour expresses itself at a later age through consciously chosen behaviour exemplified by the oral fixation of alcoholism. What makes the theory so original is that it is claimed that the conscious choice of behaviour has its origins in the repressed depths of the unconscious mind.

Proponents of the theory claim that this repression can be released through psychodynamic counselling. This counselling may be needed in a situation when the individual has experienced a physical and/or emotional crisis during their development.

Crises leading to fixated behaviour can occur at any stage of development. According to Freud, this personal development directs the individual in the direction of one of two forces, either towards 'Thanatos' or 'Eros'. Eros, the Greek god of love is interpreted by Freudians as contributing to an individual's optimism. Thanatos, the Greek personification of death is perceived as contributing to an individual's sense of pessimism. How one develops determines whether one's conscious frame of mind directs the individual to the good or otherwise. It can be argued that Freud's legacy is to have left one of the most influential psychological theories to contribute to the discipline. It is, however, important to recognize that just because the theory is famous does not mean it is correct. This point will be developed later in the chapter.

Cognitive theory

Cognitive psychology can be understood as being a branch of psychology that is interested in what happens after a stimulus but before a response. It is a school of psychology that has become associated with the work of Jean Piaget and Lev Vygotsky. We have already considered Piaget and Vygotsky's work in Chapter 4 in our discussion of the Plowden Report (1967). Malim and Birch (1998, p.27) argue that Piaget is 'the most significant figure in the study of cognitive development'. Piaget's model of cognitive development has become particularly influential within psychology. According to Piaget, the human mind develops over time as an individual is stimulated by its surroundings. From the ages of 0 to 2, the child has basic thoughts or 'schemata'. Piaget claims that these initial thoughts are limited and instinctive. A baby has a 'crying schema', a 'grasping schema' and a 'feeding schema'. These thought processes develop from the age of two as the infant becomes capable of speech and develops what Piaget phrases as 'symbolic thought'. It is also proposed that between the ages of two to seven, the child's problem solving skills are limited because of two terms Piaget phrases as 'centration' and 'egocentrism'. By 'centration' Piaget means that the child can see one aspect of a situation's reality but not the total picture. As an example, a child between the ages of two and seven may think that a ton of lead is heavier than a ton of feathers because they 'centrate' or focus on one aspect of the problem. The child assumes that lead is a metal and therefore heavier than 'fluffy' feathers. The consequence may be that the child does not see that in fact both quantities are the same weight. By 'egocentrism' Piaget means that a child cannot see the true nature of a problem because problem solving occurs in relation to what the child knows about reality. As an example, if a child aged two and seven is asked what noise a reindeer makes they may say 'clip clop' instead of 'I don't know'. This is due to egocentrism. The child thinks that the reindeer looks like a horse and knows that a horse makes a 'clip clop' sound, so it assumes that reindeer also make a 'clip clop' sound. Piaget claims that in order to progress through this stage of development, the child needs to interact with its environment through play.

As a consequence of linguistic development, the infant becomes capable of more complex thought so that by seven years of age the preoperational stage has ended and the child is able to complete complex problem solving. This stage of development is phrased 'concrete operations'. This is because Piaget claims that children aged between seven and eleven need to use props if they are to complete problem solving activities. From seven to eleven, a child can calculate that three apples + two apples add up to make five apples but Piaget claims that the child needs to have the actual apples present if they are to complete the calculation. As this interaction occurs, the child will develop what Piaget phrases as 'reversible thinking'. This is the final stage of cognitive development occurring around eleven years of age. Once reversible thought has been reached, it is possible to 'problem solve' within the mind, without using the props that a seven-year-old child needs. When one can apply reversible thinking to solving a problem, it means that one can see within one's mind that 11 + 22 is the same as 44 − 11.

Lev Vygotsky's work may be seen as complementing Piaget's theory as opposed to being a radically different cognitive perspective (Malim and Birch, 1998, p.469). Vygotsky places more emphasis upon the social factors influencing the child's cognitive development. One of Vygotsky's central ideas is the notion of each individual having a 'scaffold' of persons assisting their cognitive development. According to the nature of the scaffold, the child's cognitive development is affected in either negative or positive ways. If for example the child's peers are interested in academic issues, this social scaffold will impact upon cognitive development and make the child more academic. If the opposite situation occurs, it leads to negative cognitive development. It can be argued that this theory complements Piaget's work because it explains why some children are 'late developers' and reach the stage of reversible thought beyond the age of eleven. Vygotsky uses the term 'ZPD' or 'Zone of Proximal Development' to refer to when an individual has fulfilled their cognitive potential. This stage of development may occur at eleven. It may occur beyond the age of eleven. What becomes critical is the influence of one's cognitive development in relation to the 'scaffold' of individuals influencing one's cognitive development.

Biological psychology

It can be argued that biological psychology is becoming increasingly important due to the recent scientific advances in particular in relation to understanding human genetics. The biological perspective places an emphasis on the link between the thoughts of individuals and their genetic, hormonal and chromosomal composition. Male and female human beings differ in one pair of chromosomes and before the infant is born the presence of a 'Y' chromosome leads to the development of testes. This in turn leads to the production of the hormone testosterone. As a consequence, males produce more androgens whereas females produce oestrogen and progesterone. Biologists such as Milton Diamond (1980) and Roger Gorski et al. (1966) have been responsible for this school of psychology gathering academic momentum. The key idea considers the importance of biology in producing thoughts. It has been discovered that the male brain is physically different to the female brain due to the influence of the hormone testosterone. According to this school of psychology, the thoughts occurring within the mind have a biological basis and differences in thought patterns are determined due to genetic, hormonal and chromosomal factors.

Applying psychology to working with children and families in order to ensure holistic practice

All of the psychological perspectives that have been introduced within this chapter can be applied to early years practice and to Early Childhood Studies. There are a number of psychological therapies and each one has the potential to improve and enhance professional practice. Moreover, if the therapies are combined they offer the potential to give holistic therapy in order to assist children with complex needs. This next section of the chapter introduces some of the therapies that could be used by practitioners working with children and families. This is one example of how psychology can be applied to the early years context in order to work together to ensure best practice.

Behaviourist therapies

One of the most well-known behaviourist therapies is called 'token economy'. The therapy is based on the principle of conditioning responses, effectively manipulating choice so that positive behaviour occurs. Human beings have complex thoughts and they are likely to choose whether to conform with or rebel against accepted social requirements. This 'acceptance' or 'rebellion' can be overt and explicit or implicit and assumed. Token economy attempts to produce conformity of response at the end of every day in which the individual has complied with what is required a reward or 'token' is offered. This token has to have appeal and value to the person receiving the therapy. If there is a lack of compliance with the programme the token is denied. After a short period of time, for example five days of compliance, the recipient is rewarded with a bigger treat or prize. Token economy is used within many nurseries and primary schools. It is a behaviourist attempt to get children to comply with what is required of them within the school environment. It is a therapy that is also used within other early years contexts, but as we shall see later in the chapter, it is a therapy that is not without its critique.

Another therapy that is available for early years practitioners is biofeedback. This therapy may be used with children who have been referred for professional help because they are highly anxious. Music, light, aroma and relaxing furnishings are combined to produce an environment that can physically relax the individual. The therapy is essentially attempting to produce relaxing thoughts within the child's mind by manipulating external variables.

A third popular therapy that has its origins within behaviourist theory is known as 'systematic desensitization'. This therapy may be used with children who have phobias. The child is made to come to terms with his/her phobia in a controlled environment. It is proposed that as a result of gradually exposing the child to the phobia in a non-threatening way, the phobic object becomes manageable and increasingly less debilitating. Once again the emphasis is placed upon the importance of the practitioner manipulating the child's thoughts in order to produce positive ways of thinking about the phobia. The following case study example outlines the ways in which behaviourism can be applied when we are working with children and families. It also reveals some of the challenges that exist when particular therapies are applied to children with particular needs. The case study heightens the importance of becoming aware of holistic practice if we are to meet the needs of children and families who have complex needs.

Case study

Michaela lives in residential care. She is seven and has learning disabilities but there has been no definitive diagnosis of the nature of his disability. Michaela is thought to have a combination of autism and learning disabilities. Before Michaela goes to sleep at night, she has a habit of getting all of her clothes from her wardrobe and throwing them down the stairs. In an attempt to get Michaela to change her behaviour, a token economy programme has been designed by the members of the multidisciplinary team who work with her. Michaela loves horses and the token economy programme involves giving Michaela a token on each day when she does not throw her clothes down the stairs. When Michaela complies with her care programme, she is allowed to have a horse magazine of her choice. If she does not follow what is expected of her Michaela is denied this reward. Upon receiving five tokens, Michaela is given the opportunity to watch a DVD of her choice. Some of the staff working with Michaela have expressed concerns that there are ethical problems with this behaviour modification programme. There are concerns that this conditioning violates Michaela's right to choose what she can and cannot do.

Reflective Activity 6.5

If this form of therapy does work and modifies behaviour, do you think the therapy should be applied to working with children and families?

Feedback

You could argue that being an effective practitioner means influencing the lives of children and families. As an example, a teacher needs to be able to motivate students in order to be effective. If, however, influencing the lives of children and families becomes equated with manipulating behaviour in a way that does not respect children and families, this may be seen as being an example of poor professional practice. The rights of the child are in danger of being infringed if the therapy or way of working is manipulating the child even if the therapy is modifying challenging behaviour.

Humanist therapies

The humanist philosophy of Carl Rogers is at the centre of much of what is deemed as being 'good practice' within early years work. Rogers proposes an egalitarian model of practice in which the practitioner is not aloof from the child but 'with' the child. Empathy is a particularly important aspect of the Rogerian way. The practitioner must be there for the child and prepared to be genuine and assertive. According to Rogers, a genuine practitioner can enable children's growth and development. If these ideas are combined with other ideas from psychology, this can result in excellent holistic practice.

Effective practice is realized if there is a resolution of what is referred to as the 'would/should dilemma'. Rogers considers that this dilemma is the cause of anxiety that in turn prevents child development. Practitioners are also encouraged to direct children to their 'beautiful inner self'. Rogers believes that all individuals are innately good and that it is only the tension that results from the would/should dilemma that makes the individual a less than good person. Through a genuine and empathetic relationship, it is postulated that the would/should dilemma will be replaced by an assertive awareness of one's inner goodness. Although there are many applications for this type of therapy, the generalizing assumptions that are made within humanism can mean that its application is restricted. This argument is exemplified in the following case-study example and in the final section of the chapter.

Case study

Kathryn has recently qualified as a teaching assistant and she is working with children aged seven to eight in an inner city school. Within the last few months, there has been an escalation of racial tension between black and white youths. The situation is further complicated by an outbreak of violence between Asian and Afro-Caribbean youths. As a student, Kathryn was inspired by the ideas of Carl Rogers during a 'Promoting Positive Behaviour' module and she bases her teaching approach upon the principles of client-centred therapy. Within one of her first teaching sessions with a young Asian boy, Kathryn is devastated when the child runs out of the classroom when she is reading a story to the children. Kathryn realizes that her values are very different from the values of this child and that this limits the application of client-centred therapy. In the past, she has found that this therapy works with white children who seem to share many of her values but it is an altogether different challenge applying these ideas in this particular context.

Reflective Activity 6.6

Do you think that Rogerian therapy is more likely to work with younger or older children if we are to apply holistic practice when we are working with children and families?

Feedback

In the UK, 'early years' is associated with working with children aged from 0 to 8 years. Although it is difficult to generalize, it may be the case that younger children (who are eight years and below) are more likely to respond better to Rogerian therapy. As children grow towards adolescence, they need to develop their own personality. This may mean that they prefer to develop their own ideas and that they challenge the suggestions of others as this is regarded as 'limiting' their personal development. In contrast, younger children may see adults as being so important that they want to imitate their behaviour in order to 'please'. This may mean that it is easier to apply Rogerian therapy with these younger children. By being aware of these differences, you are more likely to be able to apply best practice when you are working with children and families in education, health and care.

Psychodynamic therapies

The psychodynamic model of the mind holds that conscious thoughts are influenced by the unconscious mind. Therapy involves releasing what is being unconsciously repressed. This then enables the individual to deal with these thoughts within the conscious mind. The psychodynamic therapist is responsible for interpreting what is within the individual's unconscious mind by analysing dreams and/or using hypnotherapy. Dream and fantasy analysis become a means of interpreting what is being repressed. It is considered to be imperative for repressed unconscious thoughts to be released into the conscious mind in order to lessen the effects of repression. The Freudian model holds that fixated behaviour has its basis in repression so that the critical role of the therapist is one of releasing repressed thoughts and then recommending ways of consciously dealing with these thoughts.

It can be argued that the psychodynamic model of therapy is hierarchical as opposed to being equalitarian. The omniscient therapist is in a position of power over his/her clients, a characteristic that can be deemed as being opposed to the equalitarian approach of Carl Rogers. This has consequences for the situations in which the therapy can be used and the clients upon whom the therapy should be used. This critique of psychodynamic therapy is exemplified in the subsequent case study.

Case study

Nathan is six and he has not attended school for over five months because he suffers from extreme 'panic attacks'. He does not know why he experiences these panic attacks but he says that whenever he thinks about going to school, he is unable to eat and that he has 'butterflies' in his stomach. Since there is no conscious explanation for his panic attacks, Nathan's psychiatrist has recommended a number of hypnotherapy sessions in order to identify if there is an unconscious repressed reason for Nathan's behaviour. Under hypnosis, Nathan talks about his anxieties about school, in particular his fear of some of the older pupils and of a recent incident when an older boy physically assaulted him in the school yard. Nathan had never disclosed this incident to anyone before and this was thought to be a major benefit of the hypnotherapy sessions. When Nathan was asked about this incident after his hypnotherapy had finished, he said that this wasn't the main reason for his fear of school and that he still did not know why he was having his panic attacks. This was a difficulty of the hypnotherapy sessions. Although it did appear to shed light on some of the things that Nathan was repressing, it still did not explain a reason for the panic attacks that both Nathan and his psychiatrist could unanimously agree upon. Nathan's psychiatrist said that he thought Nathan was having panic attacks because he was afraid of being bullied but Nathan denied and said he didn't know what was causing the anxiety.

Reflective Activity 6.7

Why might psychodynamic therapies be criticized as being an 'enigma'?

Feedback

The difficulty with psychodynamic therapies appears to be that sometimes they work and at other times they do not appear to work. The unconscious mind is not fully understood. As the therapies involve this mysterious part of the mind, the therapies may be associated with uncertainty.

Cognitive therapies

Cognitive psychologists emphasize the importance of studying what happens after a stimulus but before a reaction. They are interested in the processes within the mind that produce thoughts, not in a biological sense but in terms of cognitive processes. It is proposed that through manipulating these cognitive processes one's thought processes can change. If, for example, a child is unable to control their anger, it may be possible to apply cognitive therapy so that this anger is effectively managed. By counselling the individual to consciously change the thought processes occurring within the mind so that they think differently, there follows a cognitive restructuring. This allows the individual to think about the world in a different way. It is a therapy relying on psychological techniques as opposed to a medical therapy. If it is combined with other psychological therapies, it can offer a potential solution to various psychological problems such as low self-esteem and inability to manage anger. The following case-study example outlines how cognitive therapy can be applied to a particular example of anger management.

Case study

Taylor is five and comes from a Travelling family who have recently settled into the local community. He has a younger sister but his father has left the family home. Taylor is becoming prone to increasingly violent outbursts. It appears that he gradually becomes angry and then attacks his mother, his sister or both. Taylor's mother has become very concerned about these outbursts. In a recent incident, Taylor screamed at his sister that he was going to 'strangle' her and Taylor's mother admitted that she was finding it hard to cope. The family have been helped by children's social care and Taylor's social worker referred the child to a cognitive behaviourist therapist who began to counsel Taylor. The therapy seemed to have some success when Taylor and his mother attended the sessions. It was explained to Taylor's mother that she must always maintain control of the situation when Taylor was having these outbursts by thinking in a non-aggressive and assertive way. When Taylor was having an aggressive outburst, he had to be isolated from his mother and his sister. Taylor's mother was told that she should go and see Taylor at five-minute intervals to ask if he had 'calmed down' so that Taylor would learn that a consistent strategy was in place to deal with his violent outbursts. The combination of anger management and applied behaviourism seemed to make a dramatic difference in controlling Taylor's violent outbursts.

Reflective Activity 6.8

What do you think is the most effective way for a therapist to manage excessive 'anger' displayed by clients?

Feedback

The above case study appears to show that anger is being managed effectively by the therapies being used. It is also interesting to see that it is not just one therapy that is being applied but that cognitive and behaviourist therapies are being combined together. This may help in providing holistic therapy in order to meet the complex challenges that cannot be resolved by just one psychological therapy.

Biological therapies

Biological psychology attempts to understand the human mind by applying traditional Western scientific principles. Therapies are based on the idea that thought processes are determined by the genetic and hormonal nature of the brain. It is also proposed that thought processes can be influenced by drug therapy. As an example, an overly aggressive child may be diagnosed as being overly aggressive because of the presence of too much testosterone within the body. This male hormone may need to be regulated by medication that lessens the aggressive impulses that are produced within the mind.

In the application of therapies based upon biological psychology, early years workers may be required to monitor the drug therapy of particular children. To give an example, it has been discovered that in some instances, placing the individual on a drug regime based on dopamine can regulate schizophrenia. If levels of dopamine within the brain determine the presence or otherwise of schizophrenic tendencies, it can be argued that drug therapies have their value within early years practice. It may also be argued that the precise link between the chemical composition of the brain and human thought processes has never been exactly established and that this psychological perspective has not developed as yet to the extent that it can offer every possible solution for every possible psychological need.

Reflective Activity 6.9

Think about each of the schools of psychology outlined in Table 6.1 and suggest how they might explain child obesity in a holistic way.

Feedback

Each of the psychological schools of thought would answer the question differently. Their answers can, however, be combined to provide a holistic response to this question. Behaviourist psychologists emphasize the importance that the external environment plays in forming the individual. Obesity is understood as being a form of learned behaviour. The way to change the behaviour is through systems of reward and punishment that encourage healthy eating and discourage 'binge eating'. Humanists such as Carl Rogers would interpret obesity as being a sign of anxiety. Anxiety is a product of what Rogers describes as a 'would/should' dilemma; in other words, an individual is not able to do what they would like to do. Resolve this dilemma and they are less likely to become obese. Psychoanalysts consider that conscious thoughts are influenced by what is within the unconscious mind. Obesity is considered to be a conscious fixation resulting from a repressed unconscious experience. It may be postulated that when the individual was a baby, they had a traumatic experience during their oral stage of development and that the conscious act of 'binge eating' is a means of releasing these repressed thoughts. The way to resolve this fixation is to have psychodynamic counselling whereby the counsellor can help the individual to resolve the conflict between unconscious and conscious thoughts. Neurobiological psychologists explain behaviour through analysing an individual's genetic composition. The implication is that obesity is a genetic disorder. The way to stop obese behaviour is to isolate and amend the biological gene promoting this behaviour. At present this procedure is talked about as opposed to being done. Cognitive psychologists would explain obesity as being part of an individual's cognitive map or thinking processes. It is a type of behaviour that comes from within the mind. In order to stop individuals from 'binge eating', it may be proposed that the individual needs to have a cognitive restructuring of their thinking processes via cognitive counselling.

This reflective activity enables us to see the benefits of holistic practice when we are working with children and families. The psychological theories offer answers to the question 'why children are obese?' in their own right. If the ideas are combined together through a holistic approach, however, they offer an even more powerful answer to this question.

The complexities of multi-agency working

In Chapter 4 we commented that The Plowden Report encourages integrated services that will ideally work with each other. Holistic practice will also be an ideal aspect of the work of these services. It is, however, worth considering the challenges that can occur in realizing a vision of multi-agency working. Not all the agencies may be able to communicate effectively with each other. It is challenging enough to know what is happening within the preschool sector let alone combining knowledge of this sector with other sectors of education. This complexity is exacerbated if we attempt to integrate the work of the health and social care sectors. The best antidote to this complexity is to think how your professional practice can combine a variety of ideas. As a teacher, do you teach in the same way all the time? Or, do you combine a variety of teaching models in order to demonstrate holistic practice? Are you aware of a number of differing agendas (not only education but health and social care agendas too)? This is another way of ensuring that professional practice is characterized by an awareness of holistic practice.

Practical task

When you are in an early years setting, take a research diary and make a note of which therapies are being applied by the staff you meet. Analyse the effectiveness of the therapies by identifying which therapies work and why you think they are working. Make sure that you respect principles of confidentiality!

We can now complete this final chapter by focusing our discussion on critically appraising the psychological perspectives in terms of their value for early years and the application of holistic practice.

Critical appraisal of how psychological therapies can be used by early years

There is no single perspective that holds all the answers to solving the problems faced by many children within early years settings. The psychological therapies that have been outlined have limitations if they are applied in isolation. This is a further justification for having holistic practice.

Appraising behaviourism

The behaviourist therapies that have been summarized can make the mistake of focusing upon external variables to such an extent that the particular needs of individuals are not met. Every human being does not react in the same way to an external response. Even complex mammals such as dolphins can defy the laws of operant conditioning by doing the opposite to what they are expected to do! There is no scientific certainty that the therapies informed by this perspective will work. There is a further difficulty with behaviourist therapies that may be summarized as being linked to the unique nature of the human mind. There are profound ethical difficulties with therapies such as token economy. It can be claimed that token economy programmes do not respect dignity and human rights. A token economy programme is essentially saying 'do this for me and you will be rewarded'. This is a power relationship and it could be argued that the child is being manipulated in hierarchical non-egalitarian ways. These critiques of behaviourist therapies limit the application of behaviourism to early years. Malim and Birch (1998, p.24) criticize behaviourist therapies because they can be 'mechanistic' and that they 'overlook the realm of consciousness and subjective experience'.

Appraising humanism

It can also be proposed that there are limitations in the application of Rogerian client-centred therapy. For the child to accept the importance of resolving the would/should dilemma, it is important that they share similar values with the therapist. The child needs to accept that the values of the therapist are important so that there can be a situation where there is a link between what both therapist and client want to achieve. There are, however, many instances when the values of the child may be opposed to the values of the therapist. This can be exemplified within a school environment in which the pupils do not want to achieve what their teachers perceive as being important. This is supported by research that has been completed on the 'chava' subculture within the north-east of England. It is also acknowledged by Anne Watson (2004) in her discussion of the failings of the wider academic curriculum within the UK. Watson argues that it is not so much that the curriculum is a 'bad idea', it is more that there is little awareness of how to unite the values of the children and their teachers. The consequence may be that if an early years worker is to attempt using the ideas of Rogers, the therapy cannot work because there is no common understanding of what is important and achievable. It is all very well to say that a would/should dilemma should be resolved, but a child can only be directed to their 'inner beautiful self' if they perceive that self through a shared sense of identity with their therapist. Malim and Birch (1998, p.803) develop this criticism by arguing that a critical limitation with humanist therapies relates to the assumption that 'self-actualization' is a principal human motivation. Self-actualization may motivate particular groups of individuals, but it cannot be assumed to be a universal characteristic of every human being at every point in time.

Appraising psychodynamic theory

It may be argued that psychodynamic therapy has as many limitations as uses. The model is not based upon a sound methodology, and many of the theoretical ideas can be challenged. It is a theory that is built upon assumptions of how the mind operates. If this is the case, it can be argued that any successes within psychodynamic theory are due to good fortune as much as anything else. A more significant critique of psychodynamic therapy is that it is a theory that is laden with negative value assumptions. The therapist is perceived to be in control of interpreting the child's problems. The classic image of the psychiatric couch can be applied to psychodynamic theory. As a consequence, there is no equality of dialogue. As opposed to influencing the therapeutic process, the individual is effectively disempowered by a therapist who tells 'what should be done' in order to resolve 'fixated behaviour'. Malim and Birch (1998, p.802) reinforce this criticism by emphasizing that within psychoanalytical therapies, there are problems of 'validation'. It may be suggested that within psychodynamic therapy, the truth is invented as opposed to being truth in itself.

Appraising cognitive theory

We have already seen some criticisms of the cognitive psychology of Jean Piaget in Chapter 4. It is a theory that may have been mistranslated and turned into an unworkable model of the mind. Can it be accepted that the human brain moves through the stages that have become accepted as integral to Piaget's model? If not and if thoughts develop through more of a process than the movement through distinct stages of development, it suggests that the potential application of cognitive therapy is called into question. A further criticism is that although one can take apart a computer and identify the microchips making up its component parts, the human brain is altogether more complex. All sorts of factors that are not necessarily conscious inform cognitive processes. This may mean that a perspective that focuses upon what happens after a stimulus but before a response is dealing with part of the picture but not the whole picture of human thought. A further criticism of cognitive therapy is that the child's challenging behaviours or thoughts are always changed to those that the therapist sees as being acceptable. Malim and Birch (1998, p.801) question whether it can always be the case that the therapist has the correct perspective on the world and that the child's cognitive outlook is in need of total change.

Appraising biological psychology

The biological therapies that are available to early years may be criticized because of what we do not know as opposed to what we do know. There is still much work that needs to be done in order to understand the hormonal and genetic composition of the brain. There is also a degree of uncertainty as to why some chemical treatments work with some individuals and yet the same treatments are less effective in another identical context. This anxiety can be combined with the concern existing over the side effects of drug-based therapy and the ethical implications this has for children. Taking a particular pill might make someone less aggressive but if the consequences are the docility exemplified in *One Flew Over the Cuckoo's Nest*, this effectively reduces the individual's life chances (Kesey (1962)). Kesey's (1962) novel *One Flew Over the Cuckoo's Nest* provides a critique of the asylum institutions. The mentally ill were placed in asylums (or special hospitals) and controlled with medication until relatively recently in the UK (in the 1980s, many asylums were closed down and replaced with programmes of 'care in the community').

There is also the critique that biological psychology is reductionist. It reduces the complex functioning of the brain to the relationship existing between genes, chromosomes and hormones. By concentrating the focus on this single area, it can be argued that there is a possibility that other variables influencing human thought and behaviour are overlooked.

Summary of key points

In this final chapter, psychology may be likened to an 'academic ship of fools'. It is a complex discipline with competing views on how the subject ought to be studied. It is a diverse discipline with a range of identifiable 'sub-areas' of interest. There are a number of schools of psychology, each of which has adopted its own model of the person. The chapter has defined and explored five major perspectives that are of use to early years workers. Examples of specific therapies have been provided and there has been a critical appraisal of each of the therapies. It may be argued that the best way to apply psychology to early years is to combine the perspectives and their therapies in such a way that the complex needs of individuals are more likely to be met. If this is done, it produces a holistic approach to meeting individual needs. This is the recommended way of applying psychology to working with children and families. If these therapies are in turn combined with other perspectives from health and counselling, there is the further likelihood that our understanding of child development can be enhanced. It may be argued that this is the best way to apply psychology to early years. The book ends with this chapter because it can be argued that psychology is a highly useful academic subject for practitioners working with children and families. As well as being able to be applied to individual children, there is the possibility of using psychological therapies with children and families in general. The colloquial phrase 'it's all just in your mind' is often used in order to explain why someone is unable to achieve what ought to be achieved. This implies the importance of psychology (or studying the mind) at a general level. It can be argued that academic psychology is as important an academic subject as can be if we are to meet the challenges of working effectively with children and families. The book aims to end on this note!

Self-assessment questions

Question 1
What are the five major schools of psychology that form the basis of holistic practice when we are working with children and families?

Question 2
How can early years workers apply the schools of psychology to help children and maximize their professional practice and realize holistic practice?

Question 3
Give an example strength and weakness of each of the psychological schools of thought?

Moving on

This chapter has introduced to the schools of psychological thought. Chapter 3 reflects on 'best practice and enhancing learning'. Try to think of how psychology can be applied to teaching and learning in early years in order to meet the needs of children and families.

Further reading

Gross, R.D. (2010), *Psychology: The Science of Mind and Behaviour*. London: Hodder Education.

An excellent textbook in terms of depth of content and analysis but the material is not always related to early years contexts.

Ingleby, E. (2012), *Early Childhood Studies: A Social Science Perspective*. London: Bloomsbury.

Chapters on sociology and social policy complement this chapter.

Malim, T. and Birch, A. (1998), *Introductory Psychology*. London: Palgrave Macmillan.

An excellent textbook that is written in an accessible way and makes clear links to applying psychology to early years contexts.

Conclusion

This book has been written for students of Early Childhood Studies. Becoming aware of 'employability' and the 'best practice' that leads to employability is a key concern for many University students. The content is aimed at developing an awareness of how understandings of best practice have appeared in Early Childhood Studies. We have developed shared understandings of best practice in education, health and social care within early years. Each of the main chapters has explored where these understandings of best practice have come from. Becoming aware of best practice enhances employability.

Book structure

The book has adopted an interactive approach by using reflective activities and case studies in each of the main chapters. This is to ensure that the main learning themes are applied to specific concerns in early years. Each of the chapters has attempted to engage the reader with issues that are relevant in understanding where our definition of best practice and employability in early years has come from. It is hoped that this book is more than a general social science textbook because the content places a key employability theme within the everyday context of working with children and families.

Chapter themes

This book has explored key employability themes within early years. The formative activities within the chapters have been designed in order to develop cognitive skills so that as well as identifying where aspects of best practice have come from, there is analysis and synthesis of practical and academic content. As well as providing an academic account of where key concepts of employability have come from, the book's formative activities have attempted to enable a developmental learning process throughout each chapter.

An important theme within the book is the emphasis that is placed on the emergence of best practice within the children's workforce. The book's theoretical concepts are based on understanding the nature of best practice within the children's workforce. The book's chapters have explored six main themes. These six themes are particularly important for all students who are studying Early Childhood Studies. The chapter content has explored the differing experiences of childhood over time and space alongside reflecting on key aspects of child development. The emergence of best practice in pedagogy has been considered alongside the appearance of the concept of educare. Inclusive practice has been considered alongside the development of holistic practice. If we are to adopt best practice when we are working with children and families in order to enhance our employability, it is essential to understand where the professionalism within early years has come from. This understanding of best practice has emerged over time.

Our capacity to enrich our understanding of childhood comes from becoming aware of different childhoods in different social contexts. The experience of childhood depends on time and space. There is not just 'one childhood'. By becoming aware of these differing experiences of childhood, we are able to learn from other cultures and other times. This in turn enriches our professional practice and makes us employable.

When we are working with children and families we need to understand how children grow and develop. Part of our role as workers with children and families is to help children to grow and develop in a way that is positive. In order to help our professional practice, we need to ensure that we apply the excellent work of key theorists who have commented on child development. Moreover, it is important to regard child development in terms of how children develop physically, intellectually, emotionally, and socially. This is a way of understanding child development, which helps us to structure our professional practice.

A key part of professional work with children and families involves educating children. There may be some teachers who consider themselves to be 'natural communicators'. But teaching is a craft. It is a form of professional interaction that is learned. We need to have humility when we are educating others. We cannot assume that we will be 'good in the classroom'. Pedagogy is a skill that is learnt by reflecting on what has worked well and what has worked less well as we have been educating children. A key part of this process in the journey towards best practice is to reflect on the type of teacher you want to be. Who will you use as your teaching 'guru'? How will the ideas within their philosophy of teaching inspire your development as an educator?

When we are working with children and families, we do not work alone. We work with other professionals through cooperation and coming together. The theme of educare has been considered within the book. We need to communicate effectively with those who are working in our area of early childhood. It is also important to ensure that we also communicate with others who may work with children and families, but in a different area of specialism to our own. This is what is meant by being committed to finding 'joined up solutions' to 'joined up problems'.

The book has also examined the emergence of inclusive practice within early years. By being inclusive we are trying to ensure that as many children and families are involved with our work as possible. We are accepting the rich and diverse tapestry of humanity that shapes our professional interaction. We ought to be 'open to anything' as long as it is positive and represents 'the good' when we are working with children and families! Through being positive and through being open to ideas, we are in turn more likely to create a diverse society that will enable children and families to develop in a way that is enriched culturally.

The book explores how we can become paragons of best practice and maximize our employability. A skilled set of professionals working within early years will ideally become aware of holistic practice. We will blend ideas together. We will select the best part of a theory and blend it with another idea about professional practice in early years. In this way we will become advocates of holistic practice, where considered theoretical approaches will be offered in order to help children and families to grow and develop. Just as it takes time to learn the craft of teaching, so it takes time to develop an effective approach to working with children and families. This effective approach is likely to emerge by reflecting on what works well and what works less well.

A blend of approaches can then be used through the application of holistic practice as we are working with children and families.

All of the chapters within the book are designed to focus upon key areas of professional practice. Handley (2005, p.5) warns against 'seeing children as objects of processes rather than subjects'. The book attempts to provide a comprehensive coverage of key themes impacting on employability and professional practice. The book aims to make a contribution to enhancing the professional development of the children's workforce. If this occurs it will achieve the highest of aims. There cannot be a more important professional role than helping children to develop. After all, today's children are tomorrow's adults and they represent the social future for generations to come.

Tribute to Geraldine Oliver

The education section of the School of Social Sciences and Law at Teesside University were greatly saddened by the death of Geraldine Oliver on 18 June 2014. A great teacher, a loyal friend and a wonderful colleague, Geraldine helped to establish the University's education section from 2005 onwards. Geraldine contributed greatly to the development of the University's profile and its reputation.

Geraldine was educated at the same primary school my own mother and children attended (St Charles' Roman Catholic school in Spennymoor). From there, Geraldine attended Durham High School for Girls. She had a great love for literature and reading. At the University, Geraldine was a very talented teacher who was both articulate and intuitive.

After teaching at Middlesbrough College, Geraldine joined the hopeful academics of the education section at Teesside University. Geraldine was Programme Leader for the BA (Hons) Early Childhood Studies and for the Foundation Degree in Early Years. As a result of Geraldine's drive and determination, both of these academic programmes have grown from tens of students to hundreds of students. Geraldine has offered each of these students the opportunity to make a difference to the lives of children and families in local, national and international locations.

As an academic, Geraldine was passionate and full of self-belief. This confident exterior at times hid another side to Geraldine's character. This kind, sensitive, humorous and gentle side to Geraldine is what I will always remember about her. As an academic, Geraldine had the potential to have it all. I collaborated with Geraldine on two academic publications on early childhood, including this book. I would like to think that these publications will continue to help our students to develop their academic skills as future cohorts of students arrive at the University.

Upon Geraldine's retirement, I continued to visit her at her family home. We would laugh together at the latest news. I would tell Geraldine that the place was not the same without her. I would also tell her about the latest goings-on in an academic world that often appears as a sublime mystery.

Geraldine Oliver was a true Christian soul. She was dedicated to her family and especially to her two sons. She was known and loved across the University. We have lost a true friend.

Dr Ewan Ingleby, Teesside University, June 2014.

Answers to self-assessment questions

Chapter 1: Different Childhoods and Best Practice (p.31)

Answer 1

The nuclear family is not universal. Kathleen Gough's (1959) research on the Nayar of Kerala indicates that there are a variety of family types so we cannot say that all families are 'nuclear'.

Answer 2

Family form is influenced by 'history' and 'location' or 'time and place'.

Answer 3

Family breakdown appears to be one of the key factors influencing children's experience of childhood in the United Kingdom today.

Chapter 2: Raising Awareness of the Developing Child and Best Practice (pp.57–58)

Answer 1

The four main areas of child development we need to become aware of are physical, intellectual, emotional and social development.

Answer 2

Communication is understood to be both verbal and non-verbal.

Answer 3

Area of development	Concern
Physical	Poverty, poor diet and domestic violence.
Intellectual	Ensuring that children are supported by other learners.
Emotional	Ensuring that the child does not have a series of 'would-should dilemmas'.
Social	Ensuring that behaviour is as appropriate as possible.

Chapter 3: Best Practice and Enhancing Learning (p.89)

Answer 1

Learning is a relatively permanent change in behaviour.

Answer 2

Advertising works by association. This means that a stimulus is associated with a positive response.

Answer 3

This varies according to the individual (for example when I teach my lessons well, my head teacher gives me a look of approval!).

Answer 4

Behaviourists believe that behaviour is based on learning.

Answer 5

A major cognitive theorist is Piaget.

Answer 6

Carl Rogers, Abraham Maslow and Malcolm Knowles.

Answer 7

Surface learning can be described as shallow or superficial as it is simply the recalling of factual information.

Answer 8

Teaching by asking (instead of teaching by telling), asking higher order questions (Bloom's Taxonomy) and using case studies.

Answer 9

Montessori, Regio Emilia and Steiner approaches to education – all emphasize the importance of children being 'unique individuals'. Children are encouraged to direct the learning process. Montessori education adopts a practical approach to problem solving with 'props' in order to encourage children's cognitive development.

Chapter 4: Enhancing Best Practice through Professional Skills (p.118)

Answer 1

Piaget observed that children moved through four stages of development and that they followed these in a precise order. He defined these as the sensorimotor stage, the pre-operational stage, concrete operational stage and the formal operational stage.

Answer 2

Learning and teaching strategies link closely to these stages of development.

Answer 3

The Plowden Report (1967) places the child at the centre of education and introduces the concept of integrated care – 'educare'.

Answer 4

Piaget based his theories on observations of his own children. It would be difficult to generalize from his work. In addition he did not fully consider the influences and impact of the environment. Not all children will reach the level of development at the exact age he links with the stage.

Answer 5

Piaget and Vygotsky.

Answer 6

Skinner.

Chapter 5: Inclusion and Its Emergence as a Key Aspect of Best Practice (p.142)

Answer 1

Integration is an attempt to give access for less-able pupils to a mainstream school.

Answer 2

Inclusion is about an equality of opportunity, providing support to overcome the challenges not just to open opportunities in school but as a whole society. There is no single definition of inclusion. Revisit the section on this discussion for greater clarity.

Answer 3

Rousseau's three key ideas central to his view of children and their development:

- The primacy of feeling and sensation and the centrality of matters of the heart.
- The basic goodness of human nature and the innocence of childhood.
- That children were not just imperfect adults.

Answer 4

The Warnock Report – 1978.

Answer 5

The Warnock Report considered integration in education. Another important issue was the recognition of the parental knowledge and the importance of including this in the decision-making process.

Answer 6

The two main pieces of international legislation that strengthened the case for inclusion in the United Kingdom are:

- The United Nations Convention on the Rights of the Child (1989)
- The UNESCO Salamanca Statement (1994)

Answer 7

Two of the important statements are:

- every child has a fundamental right to education, and must be given the opportunity to achieve and maintain an acceptable level of learning
- every child has unique characteristics, interests, abilities and learning needs

Answer 8

The Salamanca Statement recognized the important role of the parents in relation to the education of their child and that their involvement in the decision-making process should be encouraged and facilitated.

Answer 9

SENDA (2001) – The two conditions that remained as a proviso for children to be entitled to a mainstream education were:

- it is compatible with the parents' wishes, and
- there is an efficient education of other children.

Chapter 6: The Rising Importance of Holistic Practice in Early Childhood Studies (p.170)

Answer 1

The five major schools of psychology supporting holistic practice are: psychoanalytical, behaviourist, humanistic, neurobiological and cognitive.

Answer 2

The best way of applying psychology to early years is through holistic therapies that combine the principles of behaviourism, humanism, cognitive, psychodynamic and neurobiological psychology to meeting the complex needs of individuals.

Answer 3

School of thought	Strength	Weakness
Behaviourism	Acknowledgement of environmental influences on the mind.	A tendency to neglect individual creativity with external factors.
Humanism	Acknowledgement of how individuals manipulate external variables.	Rogerian theory is idealistic.
Psychodynamic	Acknowledgement of the workings of the unconscious mind.	The theory is not methodologically proven.
Cognitive	Acknowledgement of the different thought processes during human cognitive development.	The idea of stages of development is not necessarily the case. Cognitive development is more a process than a series of stages.
Neurobiological	Acknowledgement of the link between human thoughts and hormones/chromosomes.	The theory is biologically reductionist.

References

Introduction

Clark, M. and Waller, T. (2007), *Early Childhood Education and Care: Policy and Practice*. London: Sage.

Doyle, C. (2005), 'Protecting children', in T. Waller (ed.), *Early Childhood: A Multidisciplinary Approach*. London: Paul Chapman.

Handley, G. (2005), 'Children's rights to participation', in T. Waller (ed.), An Introduction to Early Childhood: A Multidisciplinary approach. London: Paul Chapman (pp. 1–12).

Petty, G. (2006), *Teaching Today* (4th edn). Cheltenham: Nelson Thornes.

McGillivray, G. (2007), 'Policy and practice in England', in M. Clark and T. Waller (eds), *Early Childhood Education and Care: Policy and Practice*. London: Sage.

Chapter 1

Allbrow, M. (1970), *Bureaucracy*. London: Macmillan.

Anderson, M. (1980), *Approaches to the History of the Western Family 1500–1914*. London: Macmillan.

Audi, R. (1995), *The Cambridge Dictionary of Philosophy*. Cambridge: Cambridge University Press.

Ballard, R. (1990), 'Marriage and family', in C. Clarke, C. Peach and S. Vertovec (eds), *South Asians Overseas*. Cambridge: Cambridge University Press.

Berger, P. (1983), *The War Over the Family*. London: Hutchinson.

Cashmere, E.E. (1985), *United Kingdom?* London: Unwin Hyman.

Chandler, J. (1991), *Women Without Husbands: An Exploration of the Margins of Marriage*. London: Macmillan.

Chester, R. (1985), 'The rise of the neo-conventional family', *New Society*, 9th May 1985.

Durkheim, E. (2002), *Moral Education*. New York: Dover publications.

Gough, K. (1959), 'Nayar, central Kerala', in D. Schneider and K. Gough (eds), *Matrilineal Kinship*. Cambridge: Cambridge University Press.

Haralambos, M. and Holborn, M. (1995), *Sociology: Themes and Perspectives*. London: HarperCollins.

Hart, N. (1976), *When Marriage Ends: A Study in Status Passage*. London: Tavistock Press.

Ingleby, E. and Hunt, J. (2008), 'The CPD needs of mentors in initial teacher training in England', *Journal of In-Service Education*, 34, (1), 61–74.

Laslett, P. (1972), *Household and Family in Past Time*. Cambridge: Cambridge University Press.

Lawrence, D.H. (1956), *Sons and Lovers*. London: Heinemann.

Leach, E. (1997), *A Runaway World*. London: BBC Publications.

Lewis, I.M. (1981), *Social Anthropology in Perspective*. London: Penguin Books.

Marshall, G. (1994), *Oxford Dictionary of Sociology*. Oxford: Oxford University Press.

Morgan, D. (1986), 'Gender', in R. Burgess (ed.), *Key Variables in Social Investigation*. London: Routledge & Kegan Paul.

Murdock, G.P. (1949), *Social Structure*. New York: Macmillan Press.

Orwell, G. (1949), *Nineteen Eighty-Four*. London: Penguin Books Ltd.

Parton, N. (2005), *Safeguarding Children: Early Intervention and Surveillance in Late Modern Society*. London: Palgrave Macmillan.

Rapoport, R. (1978), *Families in Britain*. London: Kegan Paul.

Social Trends. London: Palgrave Macmillan.

Social Trends No. 40 2006. ONS: London.

Social Trends No. 40 2009. ONS: London.

Social Trends No. 40 2010. ONS: London.

Social Trends No. 40 2012. ONS: London.

Taylor, P., Richardson, J., Yeo, A., Marsh, I., Trobe, K. and Pilkington, A. (2004), *Sociology in Focus*. Ormskirk: Causeway Press.

Weber, M. (1968), *Economy and Society: An Outline of Interpretive Sociology*. New York: Bedminster Press.

Whitehead, P. (2010), 'Social theory and probation: Exploring organisational complexity within a modernising context', *Social and Public Policy Review*, 4, (4), 15–33.

Chapter 2

Alcock, C., Payne, S. and Sullivan, M. (2000), *Introducing Social Policy*. Harlow: Prentice Hall.

Argyle, M. (1988), *Bodily Communication*. London: Methuen.

Argyle, M. and Colman, A.M. (1995), *Social Psychology*. London: Longman.

Barnados (2014), Child Poverty Statistics and Facts. Online [Accessed 28 February 2014]. Available at: http://www.barnardos.org.uk/what_we_do/our_projects/child_poverty/child_poverty_what_is_poverty/child_poverty_statistics_facts.htm

Coffield, F., Moseley, D., Hall, E. and Ecclestone, K. (2004), *Learning Styles and Pedagogy in Post-16 Learning A Systematic and Critical Review*. London: Learning and Skills Research Centre.

Gardner, H. (1984), *Frames of Mind: The Theory of Multiple Intelligence*. New York: Basic Books.

Gardner, H. (1993), *Multiple Intelligences: The Theory in Practice*. New York: Basic Books Limited.

Gardner, H. (2000), *Intelligence Reframed: Multiple Intelligences for the 21st Century*. New York: Basic Books.

Health & Social Care Information Centre (2014), Statistics on Obesity, Physical Activity and Diet – England, 2014. Online [Accessed 28 February 2014]. Available at: http://www.hscic.gov.uk/catalogue/PUB13648

Hirst, P. and Woolley, P. (1982), *Social Relations and Human Attributes*. London: Routledge.

Horn, P. (1997), *The Victorian Town Child*. Stroud: Sutton.

Koprowska, J. (2005), *Communication and Interpersonal Skills in Social Work*. Essex: Learning Matters.

Knapp, M. and Daly, J.A. (2011), *The Sage Handbook of Interpersonal Communication*. London: Sage.

Lawrence, D.H. (1992), *Sons and Lovers*. London: Wordsworth Editions.

Lucas, N. (2007), 'The in-service training of adult literacy, numeracy, and English for speakers of other languages: The challenges of a "standards led model"', *Journal of In-Service Education*, 33 (1), 125–142.

Mental Health Foundation (2014), Mental Health Statistics. Online [Accessed 12 March 2014]. Available at: http://www.mentalhealth.org.uk/help-information/mental-health-statistics/

NSPCC (2014), Statistics about Domestic Violence. Online [Accessed 6 March 2014]. Available at: http://www.nspcc.org.uk/Inform/resourcesforprofessionals/domesticabuse/domestic-abuse-statistics_wda87794.html Online dictionary. (Online: www.dictionary.reference.com).

Urban, M. (2008), 'Dealing with uncertainty: Challenges and possibilities for the early childhood profession', *European Early Childhood Education Research Journal*, 16, (2), 135–152.

Chapter 3

Archer, L. and Leathwood, C. (2003), 'Identities and inequalities in higher education', in L. Archer, M. Hutchings and A. Ross (eds), *Higher Education and Social Class: Issues of Exclusion and Inclusion*. London: Routledge Falmer.

Atherton, J.S. (2009), 'Learning and teaching: cognitive theories of learning', 21st December 2011. Available at: www.learningandteaching.info/learning/cognitive.htm

Atkinson, R., Atkinson, L., Smith, R.C. and Bem, D.J. (1993), *Introduction to Psychology*, 11th ed. Texas: Harcourt Brace Jovanovich.

Bloom, B.S. (1956), *Taxonomy of Educational Objectives: The Classification of Educational Goals – Handbook I: Cognitive Domain*. New York: McKay.

Freire, P. (1973), *Education for Critical Consciousness*. New York: Seabury Press.

Freire, P. (1985), *The Politics of Education: Culture, Power and Liberation*. South Hadley, MA: Bergin and Garvey.

Freire, P. (1994), *Pedagogy of Hoe: Reliving the Pedagogy of the Oppressed*. New York: Continuum.

Freire, P. and Freire A.M.A. (1997), *Pedagogy of the Heart*. New York: Continuum.

Giroux, H. (2000), *Impure Acts*. London: Taylor and Francis.

Haughton, E. (2004), 'Learning and teaching theory', 21st December 2011, available at: www.learning-theories.com.

Knowles, M.S. (1950), *Informal Adult Education*. Chicago: Association Press.

Mayo, P. (2013), *Echoes from Freire for a Critically Engaged Pedagogy*. London: Bloomsbury.

Marton, F. and Saljo, R. (1984), 'On qualitative differences in learning. Outcomes as a function of the learner's conception of the task', *British Journal of Educational Psychology*, 46, (1), 115–127.

Maslow, A. (1987), *Motivation and Personality*, 3rd ed. New York: Harper and Row.

Petty, G. (2009), *Teaching Today*, 4th ed. Cheltenham: Nelson Thornes.

Rogers, C. (1983), *Freedom to Learn*. New York: Merrill.

Torres, C.A. (1998), *Democracy, Education and Multiculturalism*. Lanham: Rowman and Littlefield.

Torres, C.A. (2008), *Education and Neoliberal Globalization*. New York: Taylor and Francis.

Tulving, E. (1985), 'How many memory systems are there?', *American Psychologist*, 40, (1), 385–398.

Skinner, B.F. (1953), *Science and Human Behaviour*. New York: Macmillan.

Chapter 4

Alexander, R. (2009), *Plowden, Truth and Myth: A Warning*. Cambridge Primary Review. Available at: www.primaryreview.org.uk

Bronfenbrenner, U. (1979), *The Ecology of Human Development*. Harvard: Harvard University Press.

Central Advisory Council for Education (England) (1967), *Children and Their Schools [Plowden Report]*. London: HMSO.

Development Matters in the Early Years Foundation Stage (EYFS) (2012), Dept of Education. Available at: www.early-education.org.uk

Every Child Matters (2003), London: HMSO.

Early Years Foundation Stage: Parents as Partners (2007), London: HMSO. Available at: http://www.keap.org.uk/documents/eyfs_eff_prac_parent_partner.pdf

Gray, C. and MacBlain, S. (2012), *Learning Theories in Childhood*. London: Sage.

Kogan, M. (1987), 'The Plowden Report twenty years on', *Oxford Review of Education*, 13, (1), 13–21.

Malim, T. and Birch, A. (1998), *Introductory Psychology*. London: Palgrave Macmillan.

Maynard, T. and Thomas, N. (2009), *An Introduction to Early Childhood Studies*, 2nd ed. London: Sage.

McInnes, K., Howard, J., Cowley, K. and Miles, G. (2013), 'The nature of adult – child interaction in the early years classroom: Implications for children's perceptions of play and subsequent learning behaviour', *European Early Childhood Education Research Journal*, 21, (2), 268–282.

Neaum, S. (2010), *Child Development*. Exeter: Learning Matters.

Plowden Report. (1967), London: HMSO.

Sambell, K., Miller, S. and Gibson, M. (2010), *Studying Childhood and Early Childhood: A Guide for Students*. London: Sage.

Sylva, K., Melhuish, E., Sammons, P., Siraj-Blatchford, I. and Taggart, B. (2003), *The Effective Provision of Pre-School Education* (EPPE). Project London: DfES.

The Education Act (1944), London: HMSO.

The Protection of Children In England A Progress Report (The Laming Report) (2009). London: HMSO.

The Early Years Foundation Stage (Tickell Review) Report On Evidence (2011). London: DfE.

The Early Years Foundation Stage (2003). London: DfES.

The Impact of Parental Involvement on Children's Education. (2009), Online [Accessed 29 January 2014]. Available at: www.teachernet.gov.uk/publications

The United Nations Convention on the Rights of the Child (1989). London: UNESCO.

United Nations Convention on the Rights of the Child. (1989, Ratified in UK 1991). Online [Accessed 29 January 2014]. Available at: http://www.unicef.org/crc/files/Rights_overview.pdf

Waller, T. (2009), 'Children's learning', in T. Waller (ed.), *An Introduction to Early Childhood*, 2nd ed. London: Sage, 1–15.

Waller, T. and Swann, R. (2009), 'Children's learning', in T. Waller (ed.), *An Introduction to Early Childhood*, 2nd ed. London: Sage, 31–46.

Chapter 5

Baldock, P. (2010), *Understanding Cultural Diversity in the Early Years*. London: Sage.

Booth and Ainscow. (2000), *Index for Inclusion: Developing Learning and Participation in Schools*. Bristol: Centre for Studies on Inclusive Education (CSIE). Online [Accessed 22 March 2014]. Available at: http://www.csie.org.uk/resources/

Casey, T. (2010), *Inclusive Play: Practical Strategies for Children from Birth to Eight*, 2nd ed. London: Sage.

Centre for Studies on Inclusive Education (CSIE). Online [Accessed 22 March 2014]. Available at: http://www.csie.org.UnitedKingdom/resources/

Clark, M.M. and Waller, T. (2007), *Early Childhood Education and Care: Policy and Practice*. London: Sage.

Devarakonda, C. (2013), *Diversity and Inclusion in Early Childhood*. London: Sage.

DfE. (1997), *Excellence for All Children: Meeting Special Educational Needs*. Suffolk: DfE.

DfE. (2012), *Statutory Framework for the Early Years Foundation Stage*. Suffolk: DfE.

Fitzgerald, D. (2004), *Parent Partnership in the Early Years*. London: Continuum.

Gilson, C. and Street, A. (2013), 'Working inclusively in early years', in M. Wild and A. Street (eds), *Themes and Debates in Early Childhood*. London: Sage: Learning Matters, 40–55.

Locke, J. (1692) *Some Thoughts Concerning Education*. Online [Accessed 22 March 2014]. Available as ebook http://www.fordham.edu/halsall/mod/1692locke-education.asp

Nutbrown, C. and Clough, P. (2006), *Inclusion in the Early Years*. London: Sage.

Nutbrown, C., Cough, P. and Atherton, F. (2013), *Inclusion in the Early Years*, 2nd ed. London: Sage.

Ofsted. (2000), *Evaluating Educational Inclusion, Guidance for Inspectors and Schools*. London: HMSO.

Plowden Report (1967), London: HMSO.

Pugh, G. and Duffy, B. (eds) (2010), *Contemporary Issues in the Early Years*. London: Sage.

Smith, G. (1987), 'Whatever happened to educational priority areas?', *Oxford Review of Education*, 13, (1), 23–38.

Special Educational Needs and Disability Act (2001). London: HMSO.

Tedam, P. (2009), 'Understanding diversity', in T. Waller (ed.), *An Introduction to Early Childhood*, 2nd ed. London: Sage, 11–125.

The Early Years Foundation Stage (2003). London: DfES.

Tickell, C. (2011), *Review of the Early Years Foundation Stage*. London: DfE.

UNESCO. (1992), *United Nations Convention on the Rights of the Child*. Paris: UNESCO.

UNESCO. (1994), *The Salamanca Statement and Framework for Action on Special Needs Education*. Paris: UNESCO.

UNICEF, Children's Rights. Online [Accessed 22 March 2014]. Available at: http://www.unicef.org.uk/ UNICEFs-Work/Our-mission/Childrens-rights/

UNICEF, A summary of the UN Convention on the Rights of the Child. Online [Accessed 22 March 2014] Available at: https://www.unicef.org.uk/Documents/Publication-pdfs/betterlifeleaflet2012_press.pdf

United Nations. (1989), *Convention on the Rights of the Child*. New York: UN.

Vakil, S., Freeman, R. and Swim, T.J. (2003), 'The Reggio Emilia approach and inclusive early childhood programs', *Early Childhood Education Journal*, 30, (3), 187–192.

Waller, T. (2009), *An Introduction to Early Childhood*, 2nd ed. London: Sage.

Warnock, M. (1978), *Report of the Committee of Enquiry into the Education of Handicapped Children and Young People*. London: HMSO.

Warnock, M. (2005), *Special Educational Needs: A New Look*. London: Philosophy of Education Society of Great Britain.

Chapter 6

Audi, R. (1995), *The Cambridge Dictionary of Philosophy*. Cambridge: Cambridge University Press.

Central Advisory Council for Education (England) (1976). *Children and Their Schools [Plowden Report]*. London: HMSO.

Diamond, M. (1980), *Sexual Decisions*. London: Little Brown.

Gorski, R., McLean-Evans, H. and Whalen, R. (1966), *The Brain and Gonadal Function*. California: University of California Press.

Gross, R.D. (2001), *Psychology: The Science of Mind and Behaviour*. London: Hodder Arnold.

Kesey, K. (1962), *One Flew Over the Cuckoo's Nest*. London: Picador.

Kohler, W. (1927), *The Mentality of Apes*. London: Kegan Paul.

Online dictionary. Available at: www.dictionary.reference.com.

Watson, A. (2004), 'Reconfiguring the public sphere: Implications for analyses of educational policy', *British Journal of Educational Studies*, 52, (2), 228–248.

Conclusion

Handley, G. (2005), 'Children's rights to participation', in T. Waller (ed.), *Early Childhood Studies: A Multidisciplinary Approach*. London: Paul Chapman.

Index